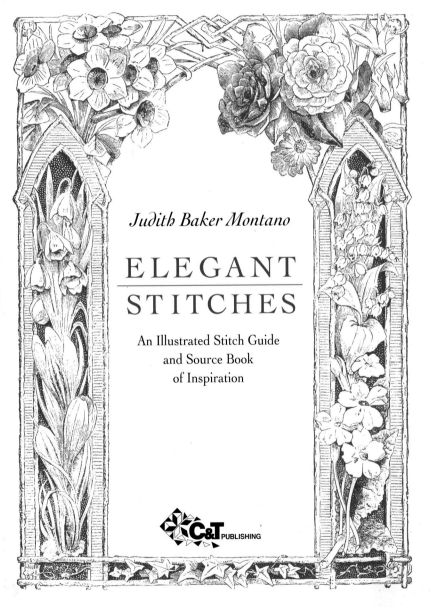

Judith Baker Montano

ELEGANT
STITCHES

An Illustrated Stitch Guide
and Source Book
of Inspiration

C&T PUBLISHING

©1995 by Judith Baker Montano

Developmental editor: Barbara Konzak Kuhn

Technical editor: Sally Lanzarotti

Electronic illustration: Micaela Carr

Pen and ink illustration: Sally Shimizu

Back cover, introduction, and free-form section design
and production: Rose Sheifer, Graphic Productions

Front cover, stitch guide, and crazy quilt combinations
section design and production: Riba Taylor

Photography by Bill O'Connor unless otherwise noted.

Kanagawa is a registered trademark of the Kanagawa Company.
Natesh is a registered trademark of Kaleidoscope.
Nymo is a registered trademark of Belding Heminway Co., Inc.
Ultrasuede is a registered trademark of Springs Industries, Inc.

Published by C&T Publishing
P.O. Box 1456
Lafayette, CA 94549

Library of Congress Cataloging-in-Publication Data:
Montano, Judith.
    Elegant Stitches: an illustrated stitch guide and source book of inspiration/
by Judith Baker Montano.
        ISBN 0-914881-85-X   p. cm.
    1. Embroidery.   2. Embroidery—Left-handed techniques. I. Title.
TT770. M634 1995
746.44'042'024081--dc20   94-44710
                                             CIP

Printed in Hong Kong

10 9 8 7 6 5

TABLE OF CONTENTS

Dedicated to Madeleine and Jason Montano (my beloved children) and to G. S. F. (who knows why).

In memory of the little boy in the navy blue sailor suit and the little girl in the red tartan pinafore.

INTRODUCTION

INTRODUCTION

Embroidery...the word conjures up so many visions and memories for me: crewel wool pomegranates flowing across an eighteenth century bedspread in Balmoral Castle; my grandmother's collection of tea towels, each heralding a new day of the week with precise outline stitches; the gift of a chain stitch horse head, lovingly made by my daughter in her seventh-grade home economics class; the delicate silk ribbon flowers that fill me with delight in the "Land of Wonder, Down Under"; the silver crane worked in silk by a Japanese student, shyly handed to me as I rushed to catch my plane in Tokyo; the look in my friend's eyes when I finished the crazy quilt landscape commemorating his parents; the assurance from my son that he loved the pink flowers decorating his new T-shirt and wore it anyway; the brightly colored yarmulkes lovingly embroidered by my friend for her son's Bar Mitzvah; concentrating on the priest's gold emblazoned robes in order not to cry at my godfather's funeral; the first time I discovered free-form embroidery added texture and life to a painted canvas; and the realization that mixing needlework techniques opened new doors. I remember myself as a young girl, the unwilling student, spending endless hours learning basic embroidery to decorate pillow cases, tea towels, and table cloths for the hope chest I was positive I'd never use. How could I know these primitive efforts would open the door to a wondrous career of teaching, lecturing, and designing, plus traveling throughout the world and meeting amazing new friends?

I've also discovered that needlework is a universal theme understood by all women. The term "ties that bind" certainly applies to embroidery. I see students in every country come together from all walks of life with the common denominator of cloth, needle, and thread. The barriers come tumbling down; laughter and camaraderie abounds. Such a small thing—embroidery—but what a lesson it has to teach! Regardless of background, color, or creed, we are all the same and I've learned this from needlework.

Whether you use embroidery to enhance the beauty of a beautiful fabric, to create an original work of art, or to simply relax after a modern woman's day, it is a technique that is here to stay—one that brings great satisfaction and pleasure.

My students are always asking me to recommend an embroidery book that covers basic stitches for all types of needlework, one that a left hander can use, and one that has some arty ideas...as a result I wrote this book. It is a basic workbook of categorized stitches you can easily work in thread, yarn, or ribbon. I've included photographs, clear instructions, and precise diagrams for those people like me who need to "see" the stitches. There's also a section for the left hander who always feels left out! For the crazy quilter, I've included a chapter on combination stitches. For the more adventuresome stitcher, there's a chapter on free-form embroidery. This stitch guide is compact enough to fit into your work basket. It has a tough cover and will prop up, leaving your hands free to do embroidery. I hope you enjoy your journey into the magic world of embroidery. Perhaps we'll meet along the way...I'd like that.

Judith Baker Montano

GETTING STARTED
WITH THE BASICS

Embroidery is a very rewarding art. It will give you years of enjoyment, but like any hobby or craft, it takes practice and patience. Start with the proper tools and materials and get to know their uses.

• **Fabrics.** The fabric acts as the background for your needlework. It should enhance the needlework, not overshadow it. Always add an extra 2" to the fabric measurement to aid handling and stretching of the fabric prior to stitching. Ask yourself these questions when choosing a fabric:

      a. Is the fabric appropriate for the subject matter?

      b. How much wear and tear will it receive?

      c. Will the threads, yarn, or ribbon work up properly on the fabric selected?

1. *Plush, Velvets, and Wools* —work these fabrics with a large-eyed needle. Use stitches that will sit up on the fabric, or the stitches may get lost in the texture of the fabric.

2. *Cottons, Polyesters, Linens, and Shantungs* —these are medium-weight fabrics and can support many types of embroidery.

3. *Moiré, Taffeta, Shot Cloths, and Satins* —these fabrics take on an old-fashioned Victorian look that's good for fancy work associated with weddings or formal accessories.

4. *Lightweight Silks, Organzas, and Batistes* —treat these fabrics with care as they are very delicate. They may need a bottom layer to stabilize them. Keep the thread and ribbon ends well concealed, or they may show through such delicate fabrics.

5. *Knits, Loosely Woven Fabrics* —some of the loose weaves may need a stable fabric on the back to hold the stitches in place.

6. *Leather and Ultrasuede®* —have the stiletto ready since every hole must be punched because of the thickness of the material. This is a tedious process, but worth the effort.

7. *Canvas for Needlepoint or Cross Stitch*—these specialty fabrics come in different fibers (such as cotton or linen) and the holes are spaced according to size (number of threads to the inch).

• **Needles.** Always have a variety of needles on hand. Be sure to use the proper needle as it will make your work much easier. The higher the number of the needle, the smaller the size and finer the needle.

1. *Beading*—a very fine needle with a tiny eye. It is strictly for beading. Traditionally, they are quite long for ease in loading the needle with beads. There are also sharps beading needles (shorter and excellent for picking up one bead at a time; I recommend a sharps #10).

2. *Betweens*—a short needle with a small round eye. Use for quilting and fine hand sewing. Common sizes are 5 to 12.

3. *Crewel (Embroidery)*—a sharp needle with a long, oval eye. Use for fine to medium surfaces. Common sizes are 1 to 10.

4. *Chenille*—a long-eyed needle with a sharp point. Use for working heavy threads, fabrics, and silk ribbon embroidery. Common sizes are 18 to 24; keep a good stock of all these sizes.

5. *Darner*—a long, strong needle with a large eye. Good for assembly work, wool darning, and working with heavy threads and fabrics. Keep an assortment of sizes 14 to 18 on hand.

6. *Millinery (Straw Needle)*—a long, narrow needle, the same thickness from end to end, with a small, round eye. Excellent for making French knots.

7. *Sharps*—a fine, strong, round-eyed needle that's rather short. Excellent for fine embroidery and hand sewing. Common sizes are 10, 11, and 12.

8. *Tapestry*—a large oval-eyed needle with a rounded point. Use for working pulled and drawn work and silk ribbon embroidery. Comes in sizes 13 to 26.

• **Threads.** The choice of thread is always governed by your choice of fabric and the project in mind. Learn to experiment with different threads and yarns to find which types work best with different types of fabrics.

1. *Brazilian Embroidery Thread*—a rayon twisted embroidery thread with a good sheen. Use short lengths as it tends to knot up. Avoid kinks in the thread by first dampening a cloth with water, then drawing the thread over it before using.

2. *Cotton á Broder*—a single, highly-twisted thread with a shiny finish.

3. *Crewel Yarns*—very fine three-stranded wool. The strands can be separated and used singly for embroidery.

4. *Filo-Floss*—a soft, loosely twisted, six-stranded pure silk thread. It can be separated like cotton floss, then used singly or in varying multiple strands as desired.

5. *Linen Thread*—a highly twisted, single thread that's very strong and has a slight sheen.

6. *Marlett*—a very shiny, viscose thread. Comes in loose strands which can be separated for finer work.

7. *Metallics*—any thread with glitter and shine is referred to as a metallic. Pure gold and silver threads are tarnishable and need careful handling, but many imitations are available. Keep a good variety on hand for couching and weaving techniques. I prefer machine embroidery metallics because they are smoother and pass easier through fabric.

8. *Natesh*®—a rayon thread with a wonderful sheen. Double it for Victorian crazy quilt stitching. It's also good for use in machine embroidery.

9. *Perle Cotton*—a single thread with a sharply defined twist and low lustre; available in plain and random-dyed colors. Often used for crochet, perle cotton is wonderful for creating texture in embroidery. Available in sizes 3, 5, and 8 (the thinnest).

10. *Persian Wool*—a three-stranded wool, thicker than crewel but thinner than

tapestry, that can be easily separated. Use for textural work in pictorial crazy quilting.

11. *Silk Buttonhole Twist*—an exquisite thread that will surely spoil you! The silk takes on a special sheen that stands up to lots of wear—plus it feeds through the fabric so easily. I use it exclusively for Victorian stitchery. One strand is equivalent to three strands of embroidery floss. For a two hundred plus color range, try the variety of Kanagawa® silk threads.

12. *Silk Ribbon*—once you've tried silk ribbon, you will never accept a substitute. The bias silk ribbon retains its color and comes in a large range of colors. It can be used in a variety of ways, including embroidery, punch needle, and covering seams. It creates wonderful texture and is very pliable and soft.

13. *Silk Sewing Thread*—a single strand of very fine thread that's used for fine heirloom sewing. Try combining this thread with other threads.

14. *Soi d' Algere*—seven-stranded silk thread that can be separated or used "as is."

15. *Stranded Embroidery Floss*—a six-stranded cotton thread that easily separates to use the strands one at a time or in multiples.

16. *Tapestry Wool*—a thick, bulky yarn, traditionally used for needlepoint. It can be used in punch needle or embroidery. Try combining it with metallics for variety.

17. *Ver a Soi*—twisted silk thread similar to buttonhole twist.

• **Stitching Instructions.** Working from the back of the fabric, insert the threaded needle into the fabric 2"-3" from the starting point of the first stitch, then work a few running stitches to secure the thread end. The running stitches can be covered as you complete the embroidery stitches (securing the thread end). The running stitches also can be taken out after the design is stitched. Work the thread end back into the needle, then work the needle through the backs of the completed stitches.

• **Silk Ribbon Embroidery.** The secret to good silk ribbon embroidery is to keep the stitches loose and even. Silk ribbon embroidery is dimensional and fast. Here are a few tips to make your stitching easy and successful:

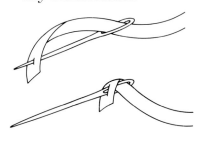

1. *Threading Up the Ribbon* — remember, silk ribbon is delicate and will fray on the edges. Use a short length (12" to 16").

2. *Needle Eye Lock* — thread the ribbon through the eye of the needle. Pierce one end of the ribbon (directly in the center and 1/4" from the end) with the point of the needle. Pull the long end of the ribbon and lock it into the eye of the needle.

3. *Soft Knot* — make the needle eye lock. Grasp the end of the ribbon then form a circle with the end of the ribbon and the point of the needle (A). Pierce the end of the ribbon with a short

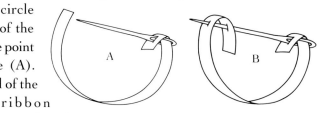

running stitch (B). Pull the needle and ribbon through the running stitch to form a soft knot.

4. *Ribbon Manipulation* — learn to use the ribbon properly. If it is pulled too tight or it twists too much, it will just look like a heavy thread.

Keep the ribbon length short, as it is easier to manipulate. Use your free thumb to hold the ribbon flat against the fabric. Most stitches depend on the ribbon being flat. Keep the thumb in place while you stitch and tighten the rib-

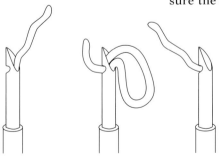

bon over the thumb. This will remove any twists. A large needle or a knitting stitch holder can be used instead of your thumb.

5. *Adjusting the Ribbon*—sometimes the ribbon will fold up on itself as it passes through the fabric, and it has to be adjusted so the full width of the ribbon shows. Hold the ribbon flat under the free thumb and slide the needle under the ribbon, then gently slide the needle back and forth (from the thumb to the needle hole in the fabric).

6. *Correct Needles*—above all, use a chenille needle when piercing through fabric; use a tapestry needle for wrapping or whipping. Remember the heavier the fabric, the larger the eye of the needle you should use for stitching.

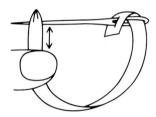

• **Using the Punch Needle.** Start out with a simple design and a medium-sized needle that will take about three strands of floss. Make sure the fabric is drum tight in the embroidery hoop or the stitches will not hold. Remember that since the design is punched from the back, it will face the opposite way on the front of the fabric. Make sure the design is facing in the proper direction!

1. Closely examine your needle. On the pointed end, one side is open and cut at an angle. On the other side is a small eye. The open side must always be facing in the direction in which you are stitching. The thread must be coming up at the top through the eye. Hold the needle much like a pencil. Relax your hand and do not hold too tight. Make sure the thread coming out the end of the handle is not obstructed.

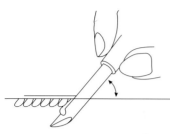

2. Insert the needle into the fabric and push it all the way down until the stitch gauge stops it. Hold the needle at about a 70° angle. I like to use the angle of the cut side of the needle as a guide. Lift the needle back to the surface and drag it along to the next stitch—about ¹/₃₂" (1mm)—and repeat. Think of it as punch, drag, punch, drag!

Do not lift the needle off of the surface. Doing so will cause messy and skipped loops. Once the thread is used up, cut it off flush at the back.

3. If you need to remove stitches, simply pull them out. Be sure to realign the fabric threads by scratching over the surface. Do not reuse the thread—cut this portion off. Outline the design in a darker shade to highlight it, then fill in with various colors and shades. Simply lay rows of punch needle embroidery down side by side. For best results, the rows should follow the contour of the shape being filled.

Like any other technique, punch needle embroidery requires practice, but it does not take long to get the stitches small and even. On my free-form scenes, I complete the piece right up to the embroidery and then punch in the grass and tree leaves through more than one layer of fabric.

Adjust the gauges on the punch needle for loops of various depths.

• **Hoops.** The use of a hoop prevents the stitches from pulling too tightly and the base fabric from wrinkling. A hoop in which your thumb and fingers reach comfortably to the middle seems to be the best (6" to 7"). Hoops come in metal, plastic, and wood. I find that a wooden hoop with the inner circle wrapped in yarn holds well and is especially useful when stitching velvet or high-napped fabrics.

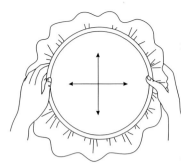

Insert the fabric into the hoop by laying the area to be embroidered over the inner ring. Align the fabric so the grain is straight and the surface is smooth. Add the top circle and adjust the tension screw if needed. Always remove your work from the hoop when you are not embroidering so the fabric isn't marked or creased.

If odd shapes are problematic, sew the shape onto a large square of support fabric first, basting the shape in place with small running stitches. Insert into the hoop. Working from the wrong side of the fabric, cut away the support fabric from inside the odd shape. The fabric is now ready for embroidery work.

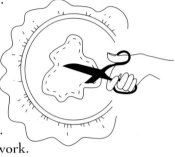

• **Frames.** Used for large pieces of embroidery, frames keep the fabric taut and even during stitching. The basic frame consists of two rollers (top and bottom) that have strips of tape or canvas webbing added across the bar length. To support the base fabric, first zigzag stitch a $1/2$" hem on the edges. Fine base fabrics almost always require support for the edges; try stitching bias tape or attaching strips of support fabric to the edges.

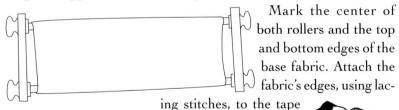

Mark the center of both rollers and the top and bottom edges of the base fabric. Attach the fabric's edges, using lacing stitches, to the tape or canvas strips on the rollers. Match the center points and work outward from the center. Roll any excess fabric around one roller. The flat side supports hold the rollers in place with pegs or screws. The overall stitching area also depends on the length of the side supports used. Attach the flat side supports, then roll the bars to stretch the fabric.

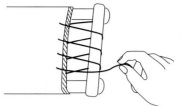

Using strong thread, lace the fabric's edges evenly to the flat side supports. Tighten the lace on each side and knot the thread ends firmly.

An added advantage of working with a frame is that it can be secured on a stand if needed, allowing the needleworker to use both hands while working the stitches.

• **Thimbles.** A thimble is a small metal cap that fits over the middle finger of your stitching hand. The small indentations on the tip hold and guide the needle into place, as well as protect your fingers! It should fit snugly.

• **Scissors.** Embroidery scissors come in many pleasing shapes and sizes. Make sure they are sharp, strong, and have long, pointed blades for precise cutting when needed. They are used for shearing, cutting threads, and cutting away excess fabric.

• **Transferring Designs.** Designs for needlework can be found in magazines, coloring books, and design books—but they must be transferred to the base fabric in order to start.

1. *Light Box*—a light box can save many hours. Simply trace your pattern onto tracing paper — making sure the lines are clear and dark. Lay the traced pattern on the light box and place the base fabric over the paper, tracing the outlines with chalk, a light pencil, or a water-erasable pen. A natural light box, of course, is as close as your window.

2. *Dressmaker's Carbon Paper*—best suited for smooth fabrics. Trace the design on the paper, then lay the paper carbon-side down on the

fabric. Redraw the design with a sharp pencil or use a ball-point pen. Be careful not to smudge the fabric.

3. *Basting through Tissue Paper*—use for high-napped fabrics such as plush, velvets, or wools. Pin the tissue paper (with the outline pattern) onto the fabric. Outline with small running stitches, then tear the paper away. Remove the basting after the embroidery is completed.

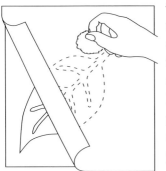

4. *Pouncing*—an old-fashioned method used for large areas. Best if worked on smooth fabrics. Trace the design onto the tissue paper, then use a needle to make little pin pricks around the design. Pin the tissue paper to the fabric. Dip a powder puff into powdered chalk and shake over the holes. Carefully lift the paper from the fabric; the design can be sprayed with a fixative.

5. *Direct Transfer Method*—if using a fine transparent fabric such as lawn, organdy, nylon, or silk, you can directly trace the embroidery design onto the fabric using a pencil or pen made for marking fabrics.

6. *Iron-on Transfers*—an easy transfer method. Use a hot iron to imprint the design onto your base fabric— remember the design reverses when applied! Always test on sample piece of cloth first; some synthetic fabrics won't take the transfer.

7. *Iron-on Transfer Pencils*—first trace the design onto tracing paper using these special pencils. Next, lay the traced design face down on the base fabric, then iron on the fabric (this method of transfer also reverses the design).

• **Pens and Pencils.** Always use a light hand when using any pencil or pen!

1. *Water-erasable Pens* — use a very light hand with these pens. As you stitch, make sure that the embroidered stitches cover all the marks. Erase the marks from the fabric back with a wet cloth and cold water.

2. *Fade-away Pens* — again, use a very light hand and be aware that the marks will fade after 24 hours. These pens work well if you need to finish your project in a hurry.

3. *White or Silver Pencils* — keep a sharp point on these pencils. I find these very successful for use on dark fabrics.

• **Enlarging and Reducing Designs.** Patterns are easily reduced or enlarged and help is only as far away as your nearest copy machine. If this is not possible, simply use the grid method. Start by tracing your original design onto paper and enclose it in a rectangle. Place the traced design in the bottom corner of a large sheet of

paper. Working from a square corner (point A), draw a diagonal line through the opposite corner of the design to the edge of the paper. Mark the desired height of the new design along the X axis (point X), then extend a horizontal line from point X to the diagonal line (point B). Extend a vertical line from point B to the Y axis (point Y).

Divide the original design into squares to form an over all grid. Now mark off the large rectangle with the same number of squares. Draw each design line from the small grid to the large squares.

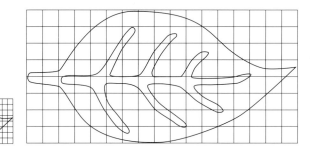

• **Washing the Finished Work.** To wash the embroidered work, use lukewarm water and pure soap flakes. Gently squeeze any excess water from the fabric, then rinse thoroughly. Squeeze again by hand, then leave until partially dry before blocking and pressing.

• **Blocking and Pressing.** After the finished work is washed, measure a piece of graph paper the same size as the base fabric. Place the fabric right side up on the paper and using the grid lines, pull the fabric into shape. Pin in position with rust-proof push pins. Cover with a damp cloth, or acid-free tissue paper, and leave to dry. If the embroidery is hard to block, or blocking isn't required, place it right side down on a well-padded board (use toweling for ribbon work) and press lightly using a damp press cloth. Do not flatten the embroidery.

• **Highlights.** Don't be afraid to collage different techniques and materials together. Once you've finished the embroidery, it may look a bit dull or sparse. Adding beads, tiny buttons, or metal findings may be the *pièce de résistance* to complete your work. Be sure to keep these highlights in proportion to your work.

1. *Beads* — small seed beads add sparkle and visual beauty to embroidery. Use them to fill in the centers of flowers or to act as individual buds. Use Nymo® beading thread for sewing them in place; this thread will not deteriorate with time or cleaning, and it is virtually invisible within the embroidery.

2. *Buttons* — keep the size of the button in proportion to the embroidery. Small mother-of-pearl buttons are very pretty with soft pastel work. Antique buttons are better with silk ribbon work on velvets or other plush fabrics.

3. *Metal findings* — small brass and silver doodads come in a huge variety of shapes and subjects. Perhaps a little bee or a butterfly will add a special highlight to your creation. Birds or flower shapes could also be used. Have fun with these additions.

• **Useful Tips.**

1. Before working the design, test your threads, yarns, or ribbons for color-fastness. Place these in a glass of water with part of them up and over the edge of the glass. Leave for ten minutes, then remove and lay out on a white paper towel or non-abrasive fabric. Using your fingers, press between the towel, then open and check for color stains.

2. Always work a small trial piece first to test the thickness of the threads, the stitches,

and the appropriateness of the fabric itself.

3. Always cut more fabric than you will need. The rule of thumb is 2" extra all around.

4. Try to avoid knots on the back of your finished work, because they cause bumps and lumps! They also show up as a shiny spots when they have been pressed. Whenever you can, run the starting end through the fabric under the area to be worked, then finish on the wrong side by running the end under the stitches just worked.

5. If you are constructing clothing that will be embellished, remember to cut the patterns larger than you'll need to insert the fabric in the hoop or frame. After the seams are sewn up, work some of the embroidery over the seam lines for a more professional look.

6. Always press your finished work on a padded board. Press from the wrong side with a damp press cloth. If pressing silk ribbon work, use a dry iron and a terry towel for padding.

• **Storage of Tools and Materials.**
There is nothing more frustrating than searching for tools or materials when you are in the middle of a project. I speak from great experience! Here are a few suggestions I've gathered from friends for organizing the projects in your workroom or those you take traveling.

1. Store your ribbons and threads in see-through containers. Whether they are shoe boxes or plastic baggies

on metal rings—get your materials out where they are visible and readily available.

2. Store your current project's ribbons and threads by color in plastic baggies. Punch a hole in one corner of the bag, then join them with a metal ring or tie them with a ribbon. Write the color code on the bag with a permanent pen.

3. Keep your needles in separate cases according to their size and use. Store one case in your workroom and keep another with the current project.

4. Keep a small pair of scissors with your current project(s) at all times.

5. Pull all the ribbons, threads, fabrics, and tools necessary for a project, then keep them in one container. I use my collection of Chinese sewing baskets for this purpose, but you can certainly use anything from plastic boxes to baskets to cloth carriers.

6. If you are traveling, a nylon cassette-tape carrier works beautifully as a needlework travel bag. The plastic sections hold ribbon, thread, fabrics, and tools, plus the pocket keeps your project clean and safe. The cases come in many sizes and I found mine at a discount store.

7. Purchase a small pillowcase or make one of calico (muslin). Store your unfinished projects in these little pillowcases to keep your work clean and neat.

STITCH GUIDE

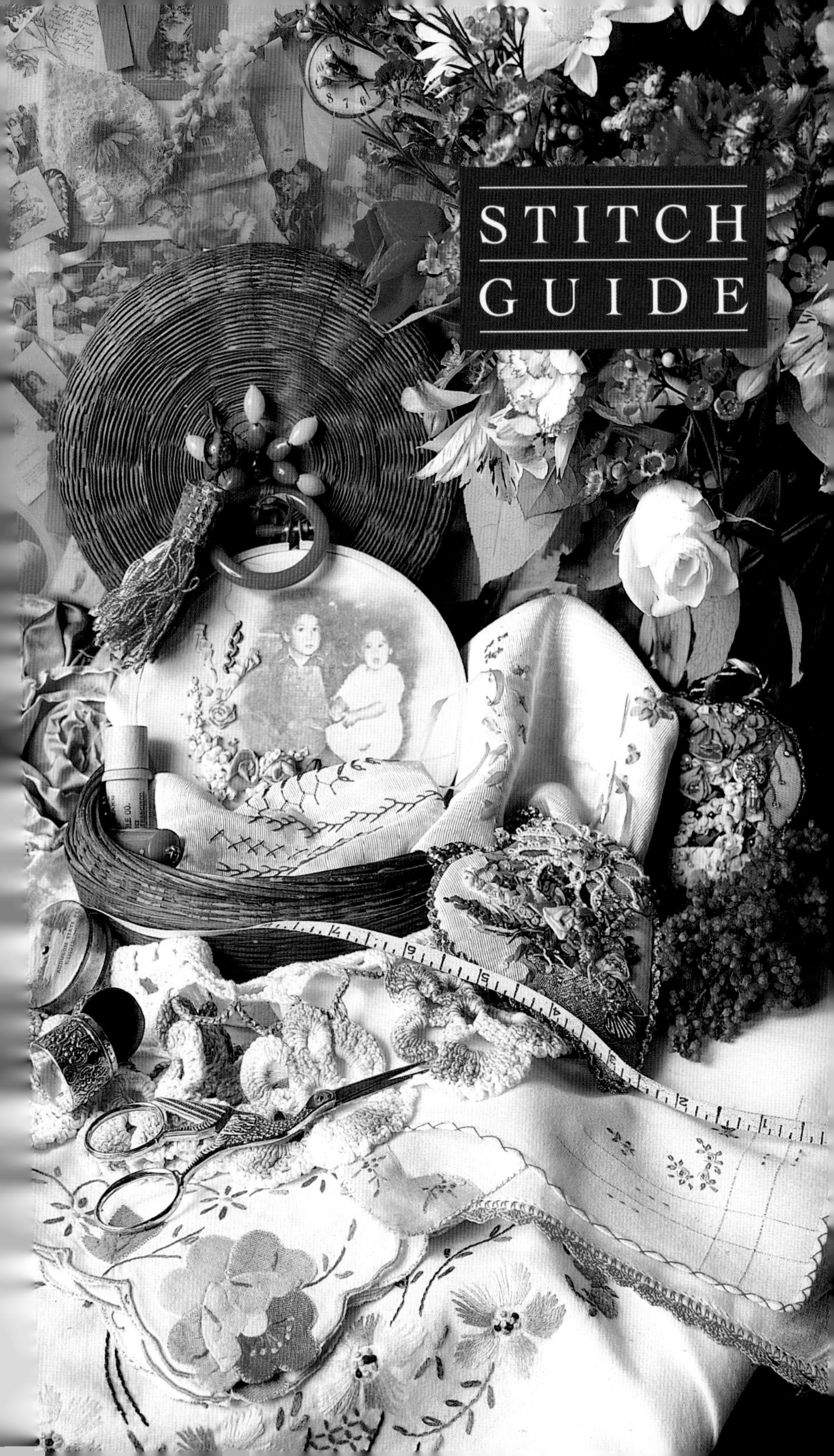

FLAT STITCHES

This group of straight and backstitches are very easy to work. You may need to practice a little to make them look sharp and precise.

Algerian Eye Stitch

Come up at A and go down at B (the center of the stitch), making a straight stitch the desired length; then, emerge at C. Point B becomes the pivot point for the stitches. Continue inserting the needle at point B and forming the stitches along the designated line until the stitch is finished. For variety, this stitch can have eight or 16 long or short rays. For 16 rays, work a straight stitch between each of the original eight; use a second color for the last eight stitches.

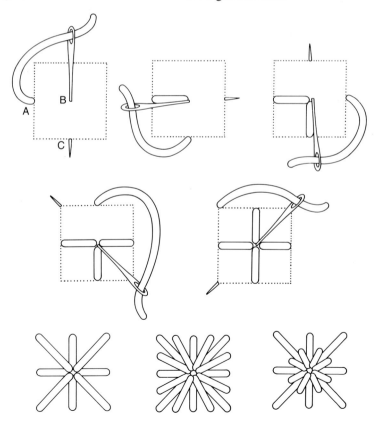

Arrowhead Stitch

Work the first row of this stitch from left to right. Come up at A, pull through, and go down at B emerging at C. On the return pass work the stitches in the same way, but from right to left, filling in the spaces—this keeps the stitches even. Use this stitch on its own or stack it to make a filler stitch.

Arrowhead Stitch — Stacked

Come up at A, go down at B, and emerge at C. Backstitch at B and emerge at D. Continue until each arrowhead is completed, keeping the stitches evenly spaced.

For a leaf, mark the shape as a guide for the stitches. Come up at A, go down at B, and emerge at C. Continue working in this manner, keeping the stitches very close and making the edge of the leaf defined.

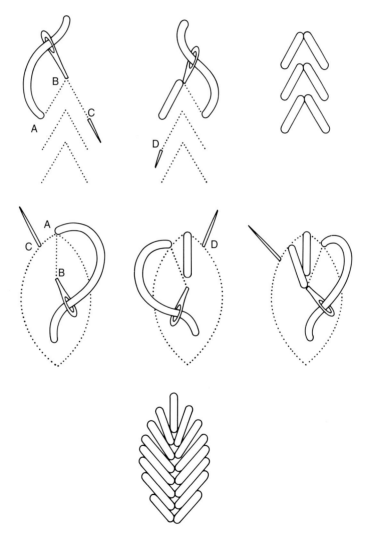

Backstitch

Work individual stitches from right to left. Come up at A, take a small backward stitch, go down at B, and emerge at C. Always move the needle forward under the fabric and come up one stitch length ahead, ready to take another stitch. Keep the stitches even.

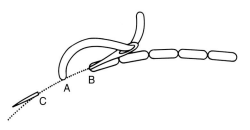

Bosnian Stitch

Work the first row of this stitch from right to left, making even vertical stitches. Come up at A, go down at B, and emerge at C. On the return pass work the diagonal stitches from left to right, filling in the spaces.

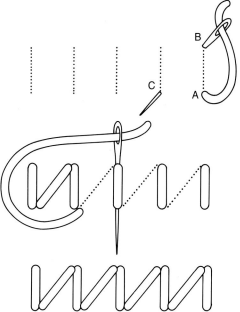

Cable Stitch

Come up at A and pull through. Go down at B and emerge at C (the center of the desired stitch length) keeping the working thread below the needle tip. Work the next stitch in the same manner, keeping the thread above the needle tip. Stitch along the designated line, using small, even stitches and alternating the position of the thread above or below the needle.

Chevron Stitch

Work this stitch, from left to right, along two parallel lines. Come up at A, go down at B, and emerge at C (the center of the stitch). Make a straight stitch the desired length to D, insert the needle, and emerge at E. Go down at F (equal to the length of AB) and emerge at G. Continue working, alternating from one side to the other and keeping the stitches evenly spaced.

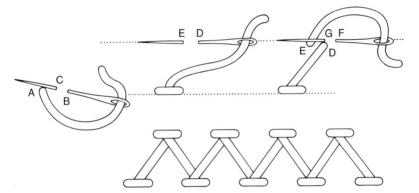

Couching Stitch

Couching is a decorative way to hold a long (laid) thread in place. Mark a line the designated length of the couching stitch. Position the laid thread along the designated line. Now with either matching or contrasting thread or ribbon, come up at A and go down at B wrapping a small, tight stitch over the laid thread at regular intervals.

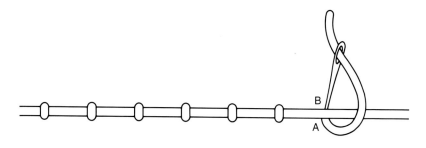

Fern Leaf Stitch

Mark a line the designated length of the fern leaf. Come up at A and go down at B, making a straight stitch the desired length along the designated line. (Point A becomes the pivot point for sides C and D.) Come up again at A and go down at C; then, come up again at A and go down at D keeping the length of the stitches consistent with the first. Continue with the next stitch, forming the stitch along the designated line.

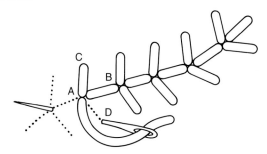

Flat Stitch

Mark two lines down the center of the shape as a guide for the stitches. Come up at A, go down at B, slip the needle tip under the fabric, and emerge at C. Continue working, alternating from side to side and keeping the stitches close together. Each new stitch will overlap the base of the previous stitch. Wonderful for filling in leaves and petals.

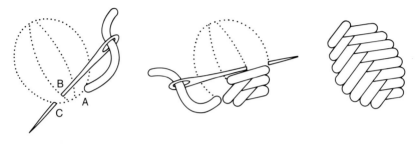

Holbein Stitch

Come up at A and go down at B, making a straight stitch the desired length. Continue working the first row of this stitch from right to left, making even vertical stitches. On the return pass work the horizontal stitches in the same way, but from left to right, filling in the spaces. Use on borders or as a filler stitch.

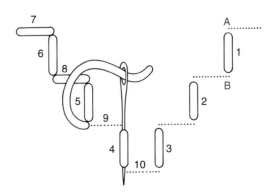

Long and Short Stitch

Mark the shape as a guide for the stitches. Come up at A and go down at B, making a straight stitch the desired length; then, emerge at C. Work the first row in alternate long and short satin stitches, keeping the outline of the shape even and defined. Work the following satin stitch rows in equal lengths; vary the thread color to add shading. Use this stitch for shading or filling in large areas.

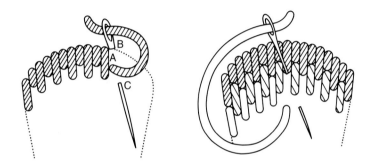

Open Square Stitch

Come up at A and go down at B, making a straight stitch the desired length; then, emerge at C. Make a backstitch at B and emerge at D. Continue in this manner working in successive rows for borders or as a filler. For variety, change the thread colors in each row.

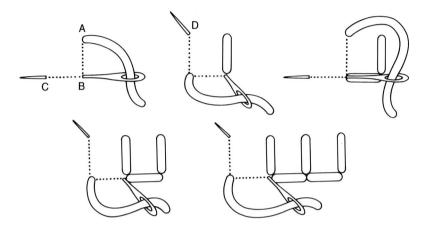

Overcast Stitch

Mark a line the designated length of the overcast stitch. Come up at A with the laid and wrapping threads. Holding the laid threads on the designated line, insert the needle at B and emerge at C, working the small satin stitches with the wrapping thread. Keep the wraps close and even. When finished, take the ends of the laid threads to the back and secure. Good for stems and outlines.

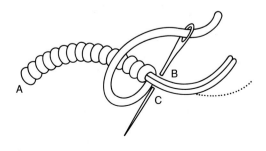

Running Stitch

Work the stitch from right to left. Come up at A, go down at B, and emerge at C, making small, even stitches while working the needle above and below the fabric. The stitches that show should be the same length as the spaces between them.

Satin Stitch

Mark the shape as a guide for the stitches. Come up at A and go down at B, making a straight stitch the desired length; then, emerge at C. Continue working straight stitches close together, keeping the edge of the design even and defined. Do not cover too large of an area or the stitches will lose their shape. The stitches can be worked in single or double layers to create a thick, smooth blanket of stitching. Satin stitches were a favorite of Victorian crazy quilters.

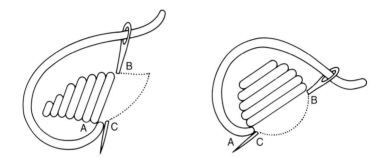

Seed Stitch

Come up at A and go down at B, making a small backstitch the desired length. Repeat for a second stitch, working the thread in the same holes, side by side. Surround the seed stitches with an outline of backstitches if using for leaves.

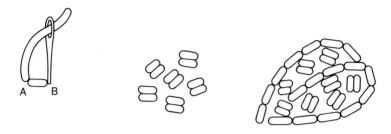

Sheaf Stitch

Come up at A and go down at B, making a straight stitch the desired length. Work two more straight stitches of equal length, evenly spaced with the first. Come up at the center of the straight stitch series and loop the thread around the stitches. Pull the loop taut and go back down at the center forming a catch stitch. For variety, change the length of the straight stitches, the number of loops, or move the catch stitch to the top or bottom of the straight stitch series.

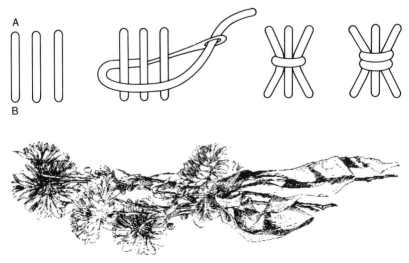

Stem Stitch

Work this stitch from left to right. Mark a line the desired length of the stem stitch. Come up at A and go down at B, making a straight stitch along the designated line; then, emerge at C (the midpoint of the previous stitch) keeping the thread below the needle. Used as stems and outlines, or laid side by side in rows as a filling stitch. When using as a filler, be sure to work the rows together snugly.

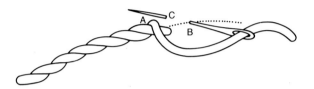

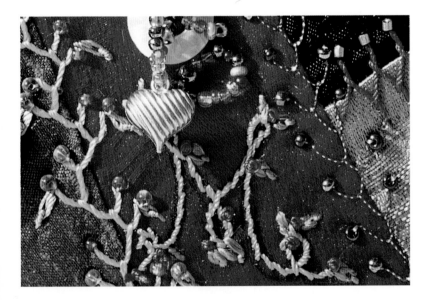

Stem Stitch — Portuguese

Come up at A, go down at B, and emerge at C (the center of the stitch). Pull the thread through and slide the needle under the stitch twice, making two loops around the stitch. Continue with the next stitch, always working to the left of the previous stitch.

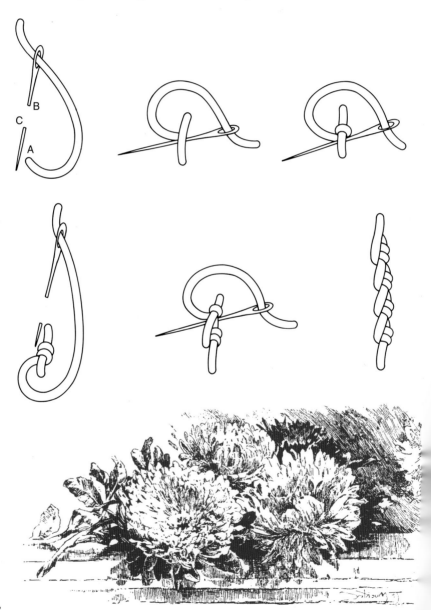

Straight Stitch

Come up at A and go down at B, making the stitch the desired length; pull the thread firmly in place. Straight stitches can be worked evenly or irregularly. They can vary in length and direction, but do not make the stitches too loose or too long or they could snag.

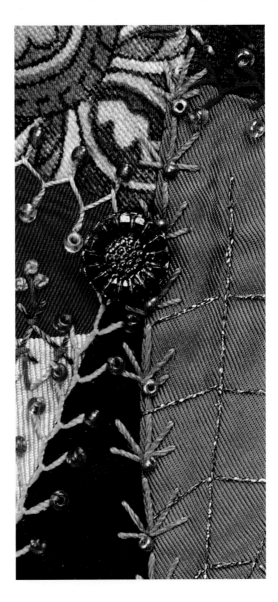

CROSS STITCHES

Very versatile and popular, these
stitches can be used individually in
random designs, or together in
rows. Be sure to cross all the
stitches in the same way to give
them an even and neat appearance.

Cross Stitch

Work cross stitches from left to right. Come up at A, go down at B,
and emerge at C, working from lower left to upper right and making a
row of even slanted stitches. On the return pass work from lower right
to upper left, overlaying the first stitches and forming an X.

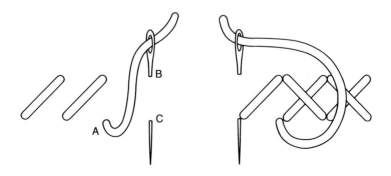

Cross Stitch — Flower

This is an interwoven diagonal cross stitch. Come up at A and go down at B, making a straight stitch the desired length. Cross the stitch with an equal-sized stitch: C to D. Come up again at A and cross over to B. Come up again at C to start the next stitch, weaving the thread through the stitches. Continue weaving to make a larger decorative cross-stitch flower.

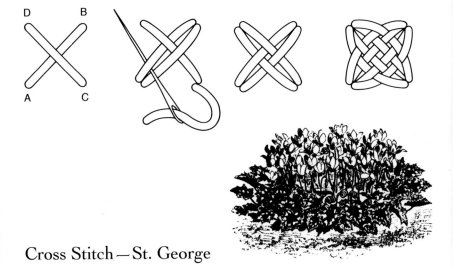

Cross Stitch — St. George

Come up at A, go down at B, and emerge at C, making a row of evenly-spaced running stitches. On the return pass come up at D, go down at E, and emerge at F, crossing each running stitch with a vertical stitch of equal length.

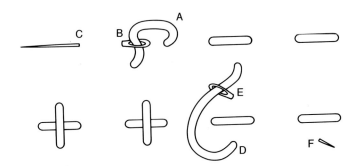

Ermine Stitch

Come up at A and go down at B, making a straight stitch the desired length; then, emerge at C. Go down at D, slipping the needle tip under the fabric, and emerge at E. Go down at F to complete the stitch. This is a long straight stitch covered by a smaller cross stitch.

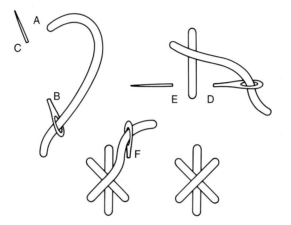

Fishbone Stitch

Mark the shape to guide the stitches. Come up at A and go down at B along the designated center line. Come up at C and go down at D, covering the base of the first stitch. Continue working, alternating the stitches from side to side and overlapping the base of the previous stitch, until the shape is filled.

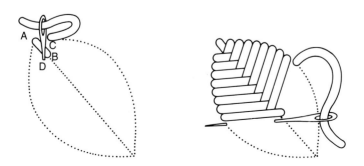

Fishbone Stitch — Open

Mark the shape to guide the stitches. Come up at A and go down at B. Come up at C and go down at D, overlapping the stitch to cover the base of the first. Work the stitches alternately over the center line to keep the spacing consistent. Continue working, alternating from side to side, until the shape is filled.

Herringbone Stitch

Work the stitch from left to right. Come up at A, go down at B, and emerge at C making a small horizontal backstitch. Continue working, alternating from side to side.

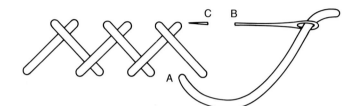

Leaf Stitch

Mark the shape to guide the stitches. Come up at A, go down at B, and emerge at C. Work the stitches alternately on either center line to keep the spacing consistent. Continue in this manner, alternating from side to side, until the shape is filled. An outline of stem or chain stitches is usually worked around the leaf.

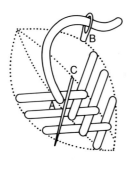
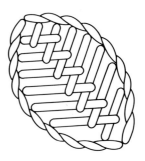

Star Filling Stitch

Come up at A and go down at B, making a straight stitch the desired length. Come up at C, go down at D, and emerge at E, crossing the stitch with an equal-sized horizontal stitch. Next, work equal sized diagonal stitches: E to F and G to H. Finish with a tiny center cross.

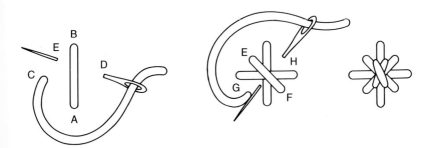

LOOPED STITCHES

These stitches are formed by looping the thread over or under the needle. The loop stitches can be used in rows or as a single decoration.

Buttonhole Stitch

Work this stitch from left to right. Come up at A, hold the thread down with your thumb, and go down at B emerging at C. Bring the needle tip over the thread and pull into place. The bottom line formed should lie on the seam line; keep the vertical stitches straight and even.

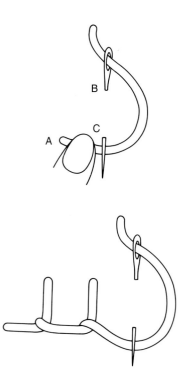

Buttonhole Stitch — Closed

This stitch is similar to the regular buttonhole, except that the top of the side stitches are worked into the same hole (B); this forms the triangle shape. Come up at A, hold the thread down with your thumb, and go down at B emerging at C. Bring the needle tip over the thread and pull into place. Go down at B and form the second side stitch.

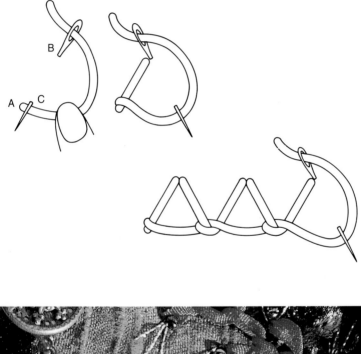

Buttonhole Stitch — Knotted

Come up at A and form a loop, wrapping the thread right to left around the thumb. Slip the needle under the front of the loop and work the loop onto the needle. Insert the needle at B and emerge at C; form a neat knot by gently tightening the loop before pulling the needle through the fabric.

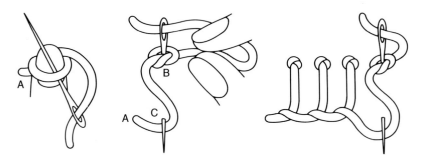

Buttonhole Stitch — Up and Down

Work this stitch from left to right. Come up at A and hold the thread down with your thumb. Go down at B and emerge at C bringing the needle tip over the thread. Go down at D and emerge at E. Gently pull the thread until the loop is tightened.

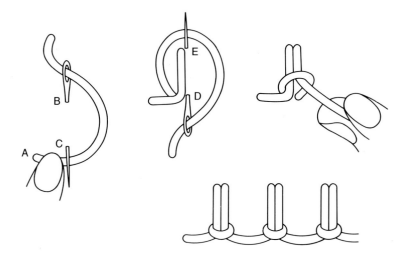

Cable Chain Stitch

Work the stitch from top to bottom. Come up at A and wrap the thread once around the needle. Go down at B and emerge at C bringing the needle tip over the thread. Pull the thread taut after each stitch.

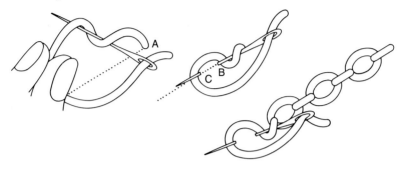

Chain Stitch — Russian

Come up at A and form a loop. Go down as close to A as possible but not into it and emerge at B bringing the needle tip over the thread. Go down at C, form a loop, and emerge at D. Go down at E making an anchor stitch, and emerge at F. Form the next looped stitch in the same manner.

Cretan Stitch

Work this stitch, from left to right, along two parallel lines. Come up at A. Go down at B and emerge at C taking a downward vertical stitch the desired length and bringing the needle tip over the thread. Insert at D and emerge at E taking an upward vertical stitch. Be sure to keep the vertical stitches evenly spaced.

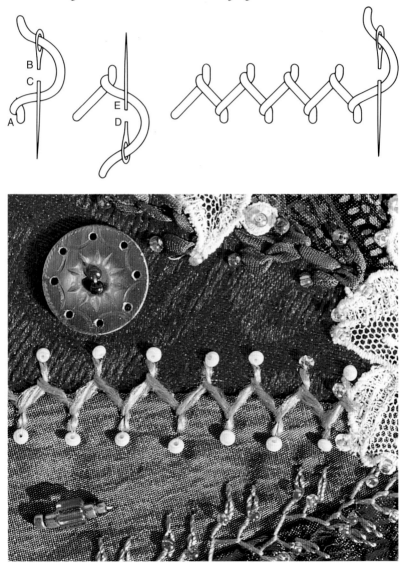

Cretan Stitch — Decorative

Work the stitch from top to bottom. Mark the shape to guide the stitches. Come up at A, to the left of center, and go down at B. Come up at C in the center of the stitch. Go down at D and emerge at E bringing the needle tip over the thread. Continue stitching side to side until the shape is completely filled.

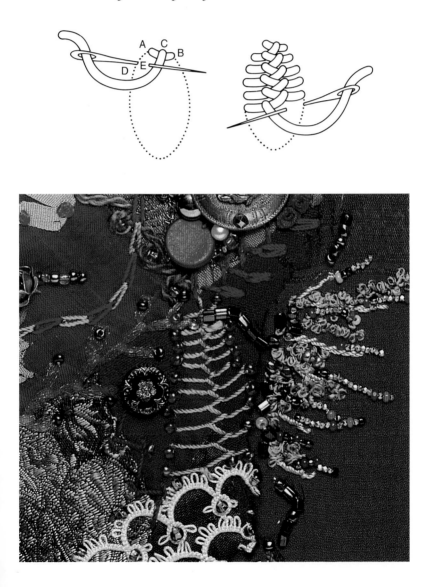

Featherstitch

Come up at A, go down at B (even with and to the left of A), and emerge at C. Alternate the stitches back and forth, working them downwards in a vertical column.

Work the Double Featherstitch in the same manner, but complete two stitches before alternating the direction.

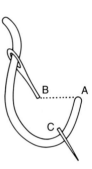

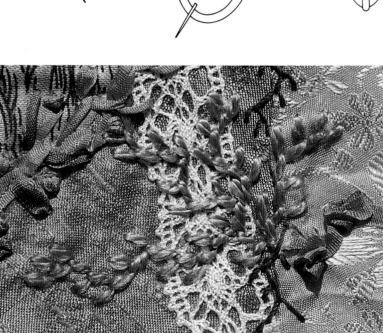

Featherstitch — Chained

Work this stitch along two parallel lines. Come up at A and form a loop. Go down at B (as close to A as possible, but not into it), and emerge at C bringing the needle tip over the thread. Go down at D making a slanted straight stitch the desired length. Come up at E and continue working the next stitch. Always work the straight stitches to form a regular zigzag pattern.

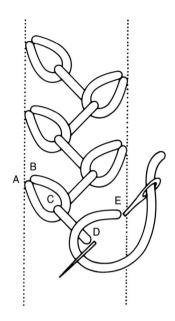

Featherstitch — Closed

Work this stitch along two parallel lines. Come up at A, go down at B, and emerge at C bringing the needle tip over the thread. Go down at D and emerge at E bringing the needle tip over the thread.

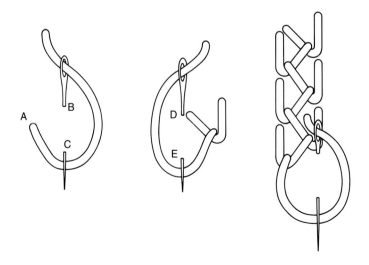

Fly Stitch

Come up at A, go down at B (even with and to the right of A), and emerge at C bringing the needle tip over the thread. Draw the thread gently through the fabric. Go down at D (the desired length of the stitch) forming a catch stitch. This stitch may be worked singly or stitched in rows.

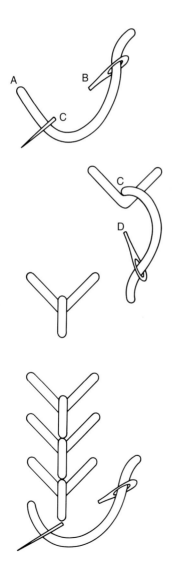

Loop Stitch

Work this stitch, from right to left, along two parallel lines. Come up at A and go down at B. Come up at C (even with and directly below B) looping the thread under the first stitch and bringing the needle tip over the thread. Continue working the next stitch, going down at D and emerging at E.

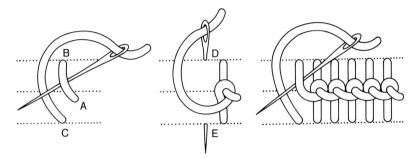

Maidenhair Stitch

This variation of the featherstitch has a fern-like quality. Come up at A, go down at B, and emerge at C bringing the needle tip over the thread. Work three single featherstitches on one side graduating the length of the stitches and aligning them vertically; then, work a similar group on the opposite side.

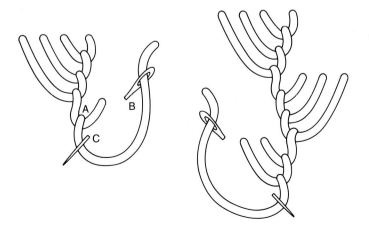

Scroll Stitch

Work this stitch from left to right. Come up at A. Loop the working thread to the right and hold it in place with the left thumb. Go down at B and emerge at C, making a small slanted stitch in the center of the loop. Tighten the loop around the needle and pull the needle through.

Snail Trail Stitch

Work this stitch, from right to left, along a designated line. Come up at A, make a loop, and hold the thread with your thumb. Go down at B and emerge at C bringing the needle tip over the thread. Vary the stitch by altering the spacing and the slant of the needle.

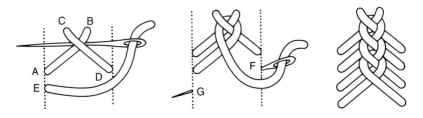

Vandyke Stitch

Work this stitch between two parallel lines. Come up at A, go down at B, and emerge at C. Go down at D and emerge at E. Slide the needle under the crossed threads and gently pull the loop in position; avoid pulling too tight or the center will be misshapen. Continue working the next stitch, going down at F and emerging at G.

LINKED STITCHES

These stitches are worked to form a continuous or meandering line of stitches. Use linked stitches to outline or fill in shapes.

Braid Stitch

Come up at A, make a small straight stitch, and go down at B emerging at C. Slide the needle under the straight stitch, go down again at D (as close to C as possible, but not into it), and emerge at E. Slide the needle under the straight stitch again, go down at F, and emerge at G. Slide the needle under the chain stitches and continue with the next stitch. Example: grains, such as wheat or rye

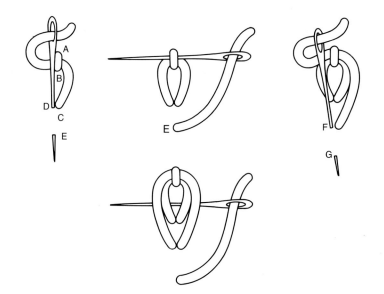

Chain Stitch

Come up at A and form a loop. Go down at B (as close to A as possible, but not into it) and emerge at C bringing the needle tip over the thread. Repeat this stitch to make a chain. Examples: stems and vines.

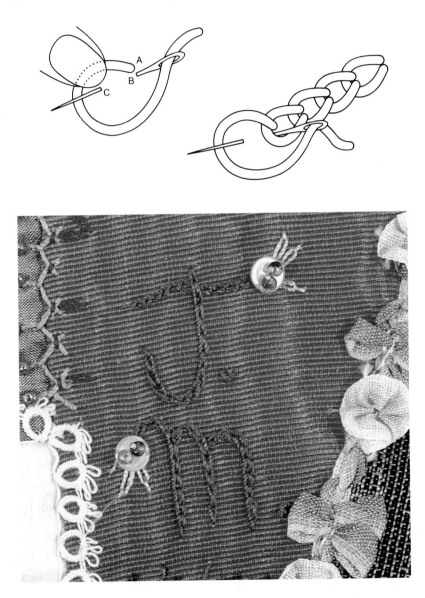

Chain Stitch — Magic

Thread the needle with two contrasting threads. Come up at A and form a loop. Go down at B (as close to A as possible, but not into it) and emerge at C looping only one thread under the needle tip. The first thread will appear as a single chain stitch and the second will disappear behind the fabric. Repeat, working the second thread under the needle tip. Continue stitching, alternating the first and second threads for the loops.

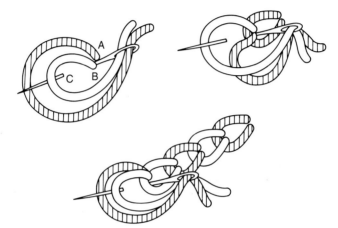

Chain Stitch — Open

Work this stitch along two parallel lines. Come up at A and form a
loop. Go down at B (even with and to the right of A) and emerge at
C (the desired depth of stitch) bringing the needle tip over the thread.
Leave the loop loose. Go down at D, over the loop, and emerge at E
for the next stitch. Anchor the stitch end with two catch stitches.

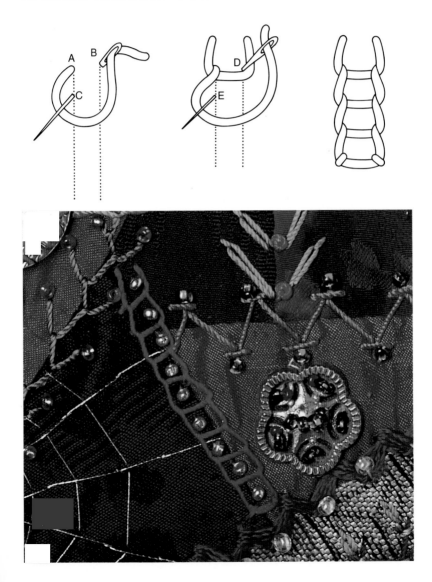

Chain Stitch — Twisted

Come up at A, along the designated line, and form a loop. Go down at B (slightly to the left of A) and take a small, slanting stitch to C bringing the needle tip over the thread. Repeat this stitch for a continuous row.

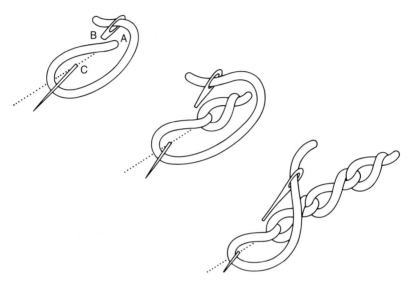

Chain Stitch — Detached Twisted

Come up at A and form a loop. Go down at B (even with and to the left of A) and emerge at C bringing the needle tip over the thread. Go down at D making a small anchor stitch at the bottom of the loop. Examples: buds and leaves

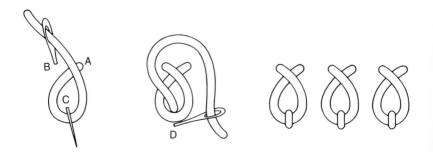

Chain Stitch — Rosette

Work this stitch along two parallel lines. Come up at A and form a loop. Go down at B (even with and to the left of A) taking a small, slanting stitch and emerge at C bringing the needle tip over the thread. Pull the needle through and pass the needle tip under the top right thread at A. Continue with the next stitch. Use for flowers if worked in a circle or as borders if worked in straight lines.

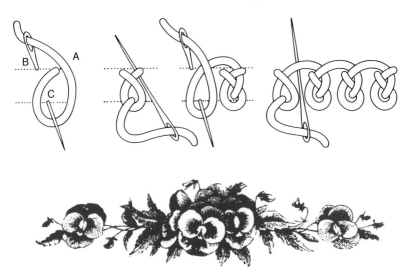

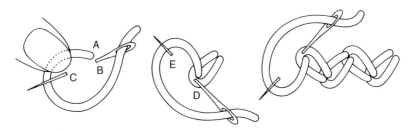

Chain Stitch — Zigzag

Come up at A and form a loop. Go down at B (as close to A as possible, but not into it) and emerge at C (the desired depth of stitch) bringing the needle tip over the thread. Form another loop and go down at D piercing the lower curve of the first loop to keep it in position; then, emerge at E for the next stitch.

Lazy Daisy Stitch

This stitch is a free-floating chain stitch. Come up at A and form a loop. Go down at B (as close to A as possible, but not into it) and emerge at C bringing the needle tip over the thread. Go down at D making a small anchor stitch. For effect, vary the length of the loop and the anchor stitch. Examples: petals and leaves.

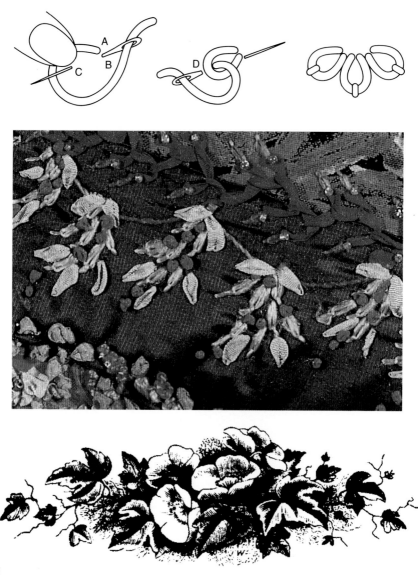

Lazy Daisy Stitch — Bullion-Tip

Come up at A and form a loop. Go down at B (as close to A as possible, but not into it) and emerge at C bringing the needle tip over the ribbon. Keep the ribbon flat. Wrap the ribbon around the needle two or three times. Hold the twists in place with your thumb and pull the needle through. Hold the twists firmly on the fabric and go down at D (you've just made a bullion knot) anchoring the stitch to the fabric. Examples: shooting stars, leaves

Split Stitch

Use a heavier thread for this stitch or the thread will be difficult to split. Come up at A, make a small backward stitch to B, and emerge at C piercing the working thread in half.

Wheat Ear Stitch

Mark a line the designated length of the desired stitch. Come up at A and go down at B, making a slanted stitch; then, emerge at C (even with and to the right of A). Go down again at D (as close to B as possible but not into it) and emerge at E. Slide the needle under the slanted stitches to form a loop, go down again at F (as close to E as possible, but not into it), and emerge at G bringing the thread over the needle. Continue with the next stitch.

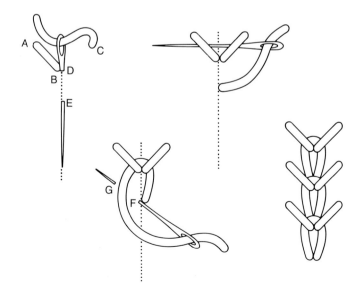

KNOTTED STITCHES

These stitches come in a wide variety of textures and shapes. They can be worked in clusters or stitched individually. Unless otherwise noted, hold the working thread firmly while twisting the thread around the needle; then, hold the knot in place until the stitch is completed.

Basque Knot

Work this stitch, from right to left, along two parallel lines. Come up at A, go down at B, and emerge at C. Slide the needle under stitch (to the right of C) and loop the thread around the stitch again, bringing the needle tip over the thread. Pull the thread to form a knot, go down at D, and emerge at E to continue the next stitch.

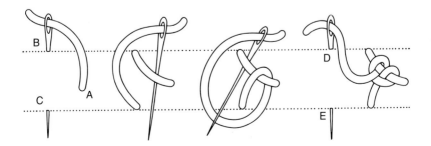

Bullion Knot

Use double thread or silk buttonhole twist for a neater knot. Come up at A and go down at B leaving a loop. Come up again at A with the needle tip only. Wrap the loop thread around the needle tip until the twists equal the distance between A and B. Draw the needle through the twists and gently pull the thread through; as you pull the thread, hold the twists flat on the fabric with the needle. Go down again at B and pull firmly to secure the knot.

Colonial Knot

This lovely little knot sits up and has a little dimple in the center. Come up at A. Work the thread to form a loop starting *over* the needle head and ending *under* the needle tip; this forms a figure "8." Hold the needle upright and pull the thread firmly around the needle. Insert the needle at B (as close to A as possible, but not into it). Hold the knot in place until the needle is worked completely through the fabric. Example: rose buds, muscari (tiny flower clusters)

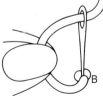

Coral Stitch

Work the stitch, from right to left, along the designated line. Come up at A and lay the thread along the designated line. Bring the needle down at a right angle to the thread, go down at B, and emerge at C bringing the needle tip over the thread. Vary the knot by changing the length and angle of the vertical stitch.

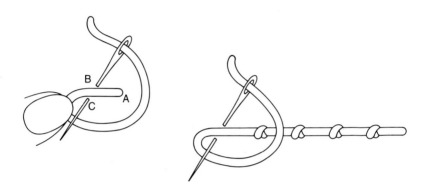

Coral Stitch — Zigzag

Work this stitch, from right to left, along two parallel lines. On the top line come up at A, go down at B, and emerge at C bringing the needle tip over the thread. Reverse the loop on the lower line, moving it slightly to the left. Go down at D and emerge at E bringing the needle tip over the thread. Continue with the next stitch.

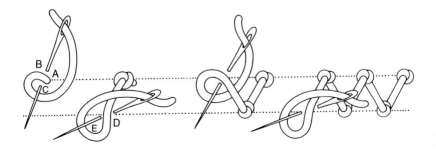

Double Knot Stitch

Work this stitch, from left to right, along a designated line. Come up at A, go down at B, and emerge at C. Slide the needle under the stitch and loop the thread around the stitch bringing the needle tip over the threads. Pull the thread to form the knot and continue with the next stitch.

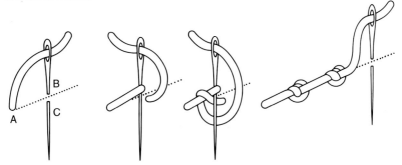

French Knot

Come up at A and wrap the thread twice around the needle. While holding the thread taut, go down at B (as close to A as possible, but not into it). Hold the knot in place until the needle is completely through the fabric. Examples: baby's breath, yarrow

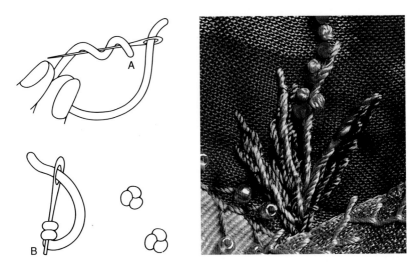

Pistil Stitch

Come up at A, allow a short length of thread, and wrap the working thread twice around the needle to form a French knot. Go down at B (the length of the short thread plus the French knot). Hold the knot in place until the needle is worked completely through the fabric. Examples: flower centers or free-form grass

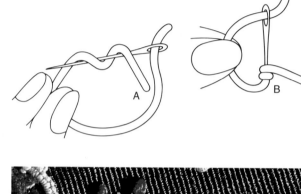

Sword Edge Stitch

If worked in lines, work from right to left. Come up at A, go down at B, and emerge at C leaving the stitch fairly loose. Slide the needle under the stitch. Go down at D and emerge at E (point A of the next stitch).

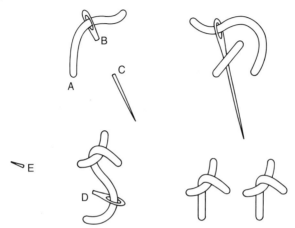

Turkey Work Stitch

Work from the top of the fabric. Go down at A and leave a ½" tail. Hold the tail under the left thumb, come up at B, and go down again at A. Come up again at B and trim the second thread tail to match the first. If making a continuous row of uncut stitches, slide a pencil under each loop while stitching to keep the loops uniform. Example: looped flowers (you may cut the loops to achieve a furry look)

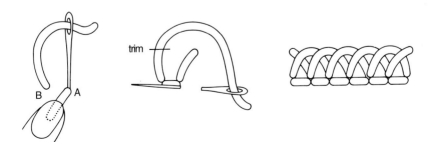

Palestrina Stitch

Work this stitch, from left to right, along a designated line. Come up at A, go down at B, and emerge at C. Slide the needle under the stitch, and loop the thread around the stitch bringing the needle tip over the thread. Pull the thread to form a knot, go down at D, and emerge at E to continue the next stitch. Space the knots evenly and close together to give a beaded look.

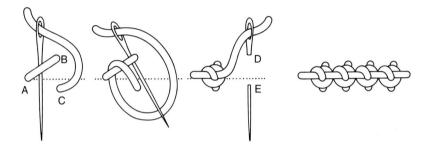

Squared Palestrina Knot

This knot is based on a square. Come up at A, go down at B, and emerge at C. Keep the stitches relatively loose. Slide the needle under the stitch, and loop the thread around the stitch bringing the needle tip over the thread. Pull the stitch snugly and go down at D. To make a continuous row, come up again at C (point A of the next stitch).

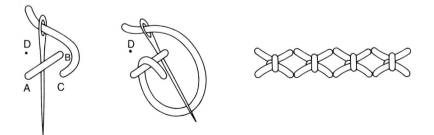

STRICTLY SILK RIBBON STITCHES

The secret to good silk ribbon embroidery is to keep the stitches loose and even.

Bradford Rose

Form the rose center with a French (page 71) or colonial knot (page 69). Working in a clockwise direction around the knot, stitch three curved whipped stitches (page 88). Work four to five more curved whip stitches in a circle around the previous round. For variety, change the shade of the ribbon from dark to light.

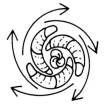

Concertina Rose

Thread the needle, using thread that matches the ribbon, and knot the end. Fold the ribbon at a right angle in the center (A). Fold the horizontal section of the ribbon over and to the left. Bring the ribbon up on the bottom and fold it up and over. The folds will take on a square look. Keep folding from right side to top to left side to bottom until the ribbon is used up (B). Grasp the two ends in one hand and pull gently down on one end (it doesn't matter which one) until a rose is formed (C). With the knotted thread, go down through the top and up again (do this two or three times). Finish on the bottom and wrap the base tightly. Make a slip knot and cut the thread, leaving a 6" tail (to sew down later).

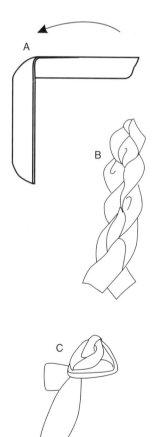

Decorative Lazy Daisy Stitch

This is a simple lazy daisy with a straight stitch added. Come up at A and form a loop. Go down at B and emerge at C, keeping the ribbon flat and bringing the needle tip over the ribbon. Go down at D forming a small anchor stitch at the top of the loop. With another color ribbon, come up again at A and go down just below C. Examples: flower buds, sweet peas, lupines

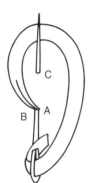

Free-Form Flower

No two flowers are the same in a garden, so relax and have fun with these free-form ruffly flowers. Use narrow ribbon, ⅛" to ¼" wide cut in 3" lengths, for tiny flowers and wider, ½" to 1" wide ribbon cut in 4" lengths, for larger flowers. Fold both ends and baste along one long edge. Gather tightly and knot the thread ends. Whipstitch the folded ribbon ends together. Leave a thread tail to sew down later.

French Knot Loop Stitch

Come up at A, make a loop, and hold it in place with a straight pin. Form a French knot center by wrapping the ribbon twice around the needle. Go down at B (close to the pin) and gently pull the knot into place. Keep the ribbon taut while pulling the needle through to the back. For variety, stitch a colonial knot center (page 69) for the loop. Examples: single florets or grouped for lupine-type flowers

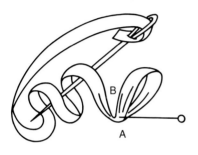

Japanese Ribbon Stitch

Come up at A, make sure the ribbon lies flat on the fabric, and pierce the center of the ribbon at B. Gently pull the needle through to the back. The ribbon edges will curl at the tip. (The whole effect will be lost if the ribbon is pulled too tightly.) Vary the petals and leaves by adjusting the length and tension of the ribbon before piercing with the needle. Examples: blue bells, asters, lily, and iris leaves

Leaf Ribbon Stitch

Mark a vertical line the desired depth of the leaf. Come up at A and go down at B, forming a straight stitch. Come up at C, go down at D (to the right and even with C), and emerge at E bringing the needle tip over the ribbon. Go down at F, forming a small anchor stitch. Continue with the next stitch, flaring out wider and wider to form a leaf. Example: ferns and leaves

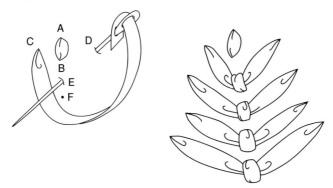

Leaves — Ribbon

Depending on the size of the ribbon, these leaves can be ⅛" to 2" wide. Cut a ½" wide ribbon 1½" long. Fold into a prairie point (with raw edges folded down to base). Baste along the wide edge. Pull the thread to gather. Make a knot and leave a tail for tacking. Tack the leaf down before the flower.

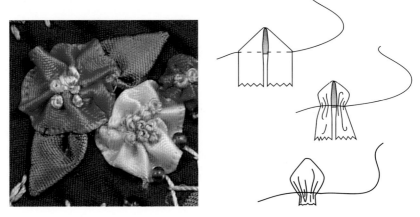

Loop Flower

Mark a small circle as a guide for the stitches and draw the points of each petal (three, four, or five). Come up at A (the center of the circle) and go down ⅛" away at B. Adjust the loop over a round toothpick. Keep the toothpick in place until you complete the next loop to avoid pulling the last petal out of shape. After completing the petals, thread an embroidery needle with floss and add French knots (page 71) or pistil stitches (page 72) to the flower centers to anchor the loops. For the larger flowers, use 7mm ribbon and a large-eyed needle. Examples: thistledown (three petals); California poppy, evening primrose (four petals); pansies, briar rose (five petals)

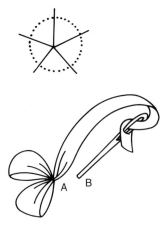

Montano Knot

Designed for the effect and not the technique! Come up at A and wrap the thread around the needle (use one to six wraps depending on the desired size); keep the wraps loose. Insert the needle back into the fabric at B (as close to A as possible, but not into it). Pull through, but do not hold the ribbon off to one side as with other knots. Avoid pulling the stitch tight; let the knot be loose and flowery. These glorified French knots are wonderful as fillers and floral sprays.

Plume Stitch

Work the stitch from top to bottom. Come up at A and go down ⅛"
away at B to make a loop—control it with a round toothpick. Hold
the loop in place and come up at C, piercing the fabric and the first
ribbon loop. Form another loop. Continue working downward until
the plume is finished. Examples: astilbe, ferns; good fillers

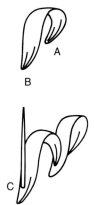

Rosette Bud

While keeping the ribbon flat, come up at A and go down at B making a small straight stitch. Come up at C and go down at D creating a padded straight stitch; do not pull the ribbon tight. Angle the second stitch to the right, covering the base of the first. Angle the third stitch to the left, covering the base of the second.

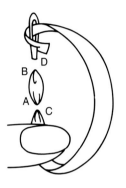

Straight Stitch Bud

While keeping the ribbon flat, come up at A and go down at B. Come up at C and go down at D, creating a padded straight stitch; do not pull the ribbon tight. Using floss or 2mm ribbon, form the leaves and stem with a fly stitch (page 54).

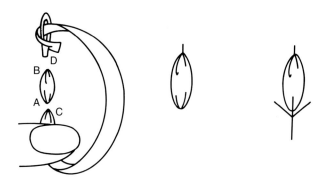

Straight Stitch Rose

For the rose center, come up at A and go down at B making a straight stitch angled to the right. Cover the first stitch with a vertical straight stitch and overlay the stitches with a straight stitch angled to the left. Now circle the center piece with six straight stitches. Overlap the joining petal points of the first round with a second circle of longer straight stitches.

Twisted Loop Stitch

This is a free-form stitch. Come up at A, purposely twist the loop once, and go down at B. Hold the loop in place and come up at C, piercing the fabric and the first ribbon loop. Use a needle or round toothpick to hold each loop until you come up for the next loop to avoid pulling the loops out of shape. Good for plumes and frilly flowers like iris.

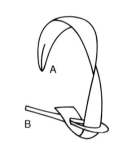

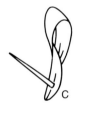

Whip Stitch — Single
(Grub Stitch, Maggot Stitch, Sausage Stitch)

Whatever the name, this is a very easy, effective stitch. While keeping the ribbon flat, come up at A and go down at B making a straight stitch the desired length. Bring the needle up again at A. Depending on the desired effect, wrap the straight stitch two or three times, keeping the ribbon flat. Anchor the stitch by passing the needle to the back. Examples: seeds, gladioli, buds

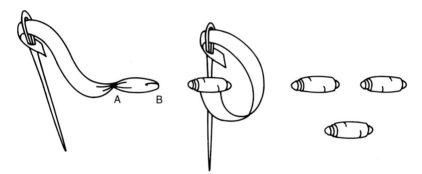

Whip Stitch — Curved

While keeping the ribbon flat, come up at A and go down at B making a straight stitch the desired length. Bring the needle up again at A. Wrap the straight stitch two or three times while working toward B and keeping the ribbon flat. Crowd the stitch so it will curve. Repeat the wraps working toward A. Anchor the stitch by passing the needle to the back. Examples: buds, roses, honeysuckle, broom

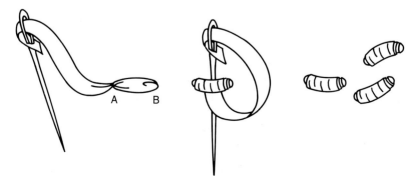

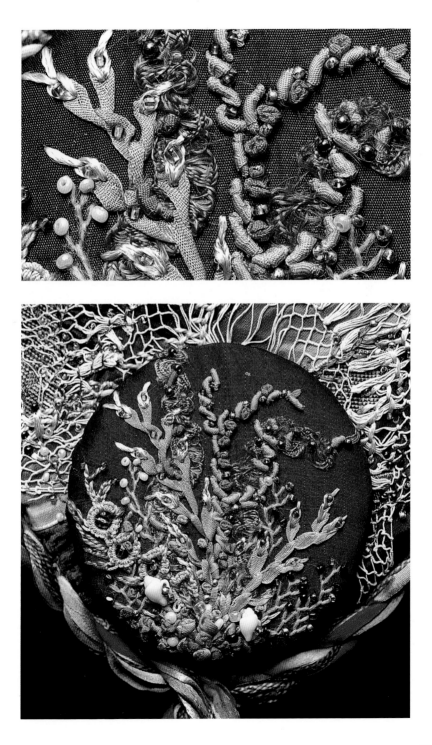

COMPOSITE STITCHES

This group of stitches is worked together to make up new stitches—perhaps two traditional stitches are combined to make a composite stitch. These stitches are very pretty when combined and they work well for Victorian crazy quilting.

Backstitch—Star Stitch

This pretty design is made of multiple straight stitches (page 39). Come up at A and go down at B (point B becomes the center pivot of the stitch). Continue stitching the spokes, keeping them of equal length and spaced evenly. After completing the spokes, connect them with straight stitches on the edges. Examples: six- or eight-spoked star, wheel

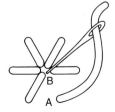
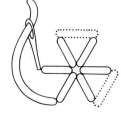

Backstitch — Threaded

This stitch is composed of the backstitch (page 27) and two loop stitches worked with contrasting threads. Come up at A, take a small backward stitch to B, and emerge at C. Work the backstitches the length of the desired line. Come up at 1 with the first contrasting thread. Slide the needle under the backstitches, alternating above and below the row without catching the fabric. Interweave the second thread to complete the loops.

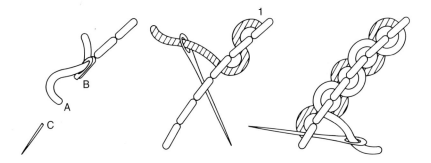

Chain Stitch — Spiny

This stitch is composed of the chain stitch (page 59) and straight stitch (page 39). Come up at A and form a loop. Go down at B and emerge at C bringing the needle tip over the thread. Go down at D, making a straight stitch the desired length, and emerge at E. Go down at F and emerge at G bringing the needle tip over the thread to continue the next stitch.

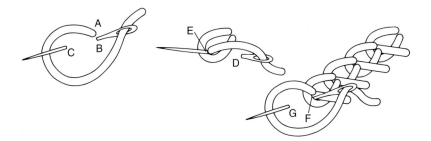

Chain Stitch — Whipped

Using a matching color of embroidery floss, make a row of continuous chain stitches (page 59). Using a blunt needle to prevent piercing the stitched ribbon, come up at point A and wrap the needle around each individual chain stitch. Keep the ribbon flat as you work.

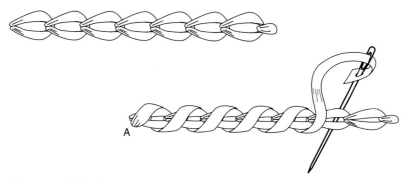

Crown Stitch

This stitch is composed of a fly stitch (page 54) and two straight stitches (page 39). Come up at A, go down at B, and emerge at C bringing the needle tip over the thread. Keep the stitch loose to form a slight curve. Form a catch stitch by inserting the needle at D (the desired stitch length) and emerge at E bringing the needle tip to the right of the working thread. Insert the needle at F and emerge at G. Insert the needle into H, to the left of the center straight stitch.

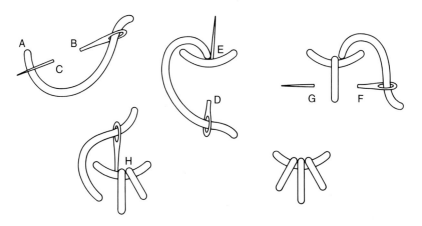

Head of the Bull Stitch (Tête de Boeuf Stitch)

This stitch is composed of a fly stitch (page 54) and lazy daisy stitch (page 64). Come up at A, go down at B, and emerge at C bringing the needle tip over the thread. Go down at D, to the right of the working thread, and emerge at E bringing the needle tip over the thread. Take a small stitch at F to anchor the loop.

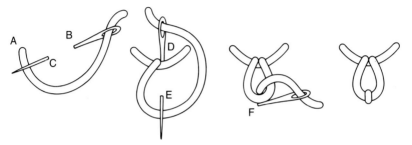

Herringbone Stitch — Laced

This stitch is composed of a modified herringbone (page 44) and a lacing thread. Come up at A, go down at B, and take a small horizontal stitch to emerge at C. Slide the needle under the slanted stitch before making the backstitches. Work a row of modified herringbone stitches the desired length. With a contrasting thread, come up at 1. Slide the thread under the first crossing of slanted stitches, and work it *over, under,* and *over* the slanted stitches. Work it *under* the thread at point 1, and then *over,* and *under* at the same crossing and bringing the thread to the lower crossing.

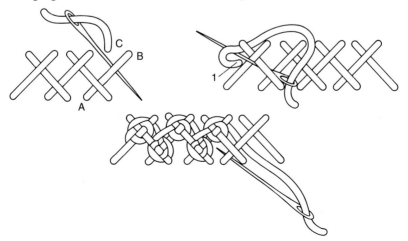

Magic Chain Band Stitch

This stitch is composed of straight stitches (page 39) and a magic chain (page 60). Come up at A and go down at B; then, continue working a column of straight stitches (keeping them of equal length). Thread the needle with two contrasting threads. Come up at C, loop only one thread under the needle, and insert the needle at D (as close to C as possible, but not into it). Emerge at E bringing the needle tip over the thread while working the loop over the straight stitch. The first thread will appear as a single chain stitch and the second will disappear behind the fabric. Repeat the stitch, working the second thread under the needle. Continue stitching, alternating the first and second threads for the loops.

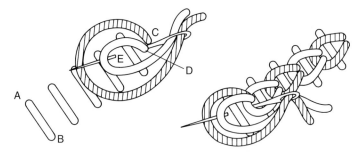

Pekinese Stitch

This stitch is composed of backstitches (page 27) and a looping backstitch. Come up at A, take a small backward stitch to B, and emerge at C. Continue working the backstitches to the length of the desired line. Using a thread of a contrasting color, come up at 1, slide the needle under the previous backstitch, and loop the thread under the first backstitch bringing the needle tip over the thread. Continue weaving the needle to complete the stitch.

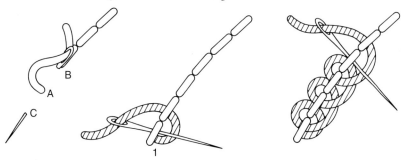

Petal Stitch

This stitch is composed of a modified stem stitch (page 37) and a lazy daisy (page 64). Come up at A, go down at B, and emerge at C (the midpoint of the previous stitch). Form a loop and insert the needle at D. Emerge at E bringing the needle tip over the thread. Take a small stitch at F to anchor the bottom of the loop and emerge at G. Insert the needle again at C and emerge at B. Work the next lazy daisy at point B.

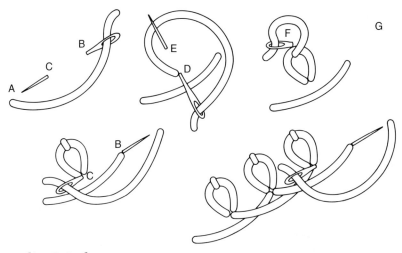

Tulip Stitch

This stitch is composed of a chain (page 59) and a straight stitch (page 39). Come up at A and form a loop. Go down at B and emerge at C bringing the needle tip over the thread. Take a small stitch at D to anchor the bottom of the loop and emerge at E. Slide the needle under the anchor stitch and go down at F.

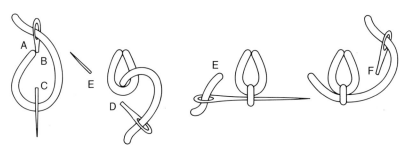

Whipped Stem Stitch

This stitch is composed of a stem stitch (page 37) and a whip stitch (page 88). Come up at A, go down at B, and emerge at C (the midpoint of the stitch) keeping the thread below the needle tip. Work the stem stitches the length of the desired line. Using a thread of a contrasting color, come up at 1 and slide the needle under the stem stitches working the whip stitches at even intervals without catching the fabric.

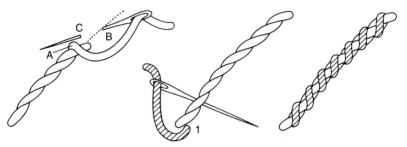

Whipped or Laced Running Stitch

This stitch is composed of a running stitch (page 34) and a whip stitch (page 88) or lacing thread. Work the stitch from right to left. Come up at A and go down at B, working the running stitch the desired length. For a whipped stitch: use a contrasting thread and come up at 1, sliding the needle under the running stitches at even intervals. For a laced stitch: use a contrasting thread and come up at 1, sliding the needle under the running stitches while working above and below the running stitches.

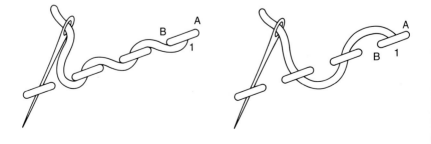

ROSES

A rose is a rose is a rose...worked in either ribbon, yarn, or thread. Keep the stitches loose to give the rose dimension.

Bullion Rose

For the rose center, work three bullion knots (page 68) of equal length to form a triangle. Now work a bullion knot to wrap around one corner of the triangle. Lengthen the knots as needed, so each knot curls around the others. Continue stitching knots around the triangle until the rose is formed.

Chain Rose

Mark a circle the size of the desired rose. Come up at A within the circle. Go down at B and emerge at C bringing the needle tip over the ribbon. Repeat this stitch, making a continuous chain and working in a counter-clockwise direction to fill the circle. Use also for chrysanthemums.

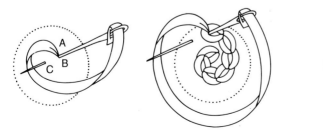

Couched Rose

Use two threaded needles—one with a dark and one with a light shade of ribbon. Come up at A with the dark ribbon and form a "U" shape. Go down at B keeping the ribbon loose. Couch the U with the light ribbon. Continue working around the center U, couching the ribbon down to form the rose. This rose works best with 4mm or 7mm wide ribbon.

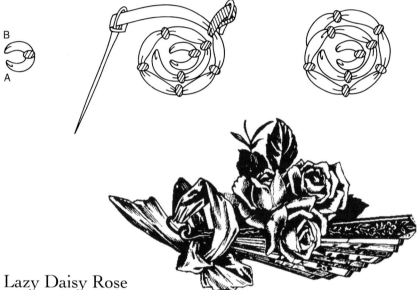

Lazy Daisy Rose

Make a Japanese ribbon stitch (page 80) the desired length: A to B. Come up at A and make a lazy daisy stitch (page 64) angled to the right. Come up again and make a larger lazy daisy stitch angled to the left. For the rose base, use a darker shade of the ribbon color than used for the petals or use green ribbon. Starting at the bottom center of the petals make a straight stitch angled to the right. Make another straight stitch angled to the left. Work the third straight stitch in the base center, covering the base of the left straight stitch.

Rambler Rose

Work a small cluster of French knots (page 71) for the center. Form the rose sides by working two or three rounds of loose stem stitches counter clockwise around the knot; come up at A, go down at B, and emerge at C. Make the stem stitch longer with each round.

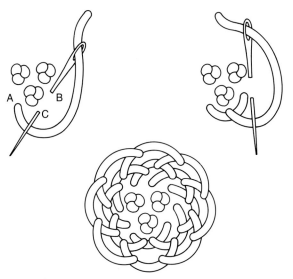

Rosette Stitch

Come up at A and make a loop. Insert the needle at B and emerge at C leaving the needle in the fabric. Pull the working thread up and wrap it carefully three or four times around the needle. Try to keep the threads lying flat and side by side. Pull the needle through slowly and insert the needle at D tacking the rosette at both ends.

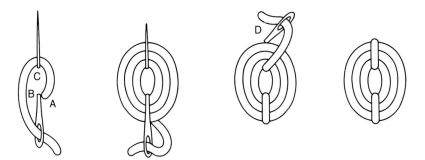

Spider Web Rose

Form the anchor stitch with a fly stitch, using perle cotton or embroidery floss. Come up at A, go down at B, and emerge at C bringing the needle tip over the thread. Go down at D, forming a catch stitch. Add a bar of equal length on each side, forming five spokes. Come up in the center of the spokes with the ribbon. Working in a counterclockwise direction, weave the ribbon over and under the spokes. Let the ribbon twist and keep it loose as you work. Weave the ribbon until all the spokes are covered.

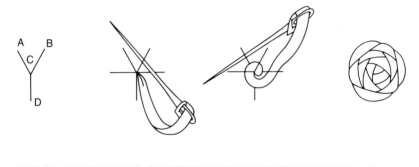

STITCHES FOR
LEFT-HANDERS

STITCHES FOR LEFT-HANDERS

At last, a section just for left handers! Study the diagrams and read the written instructions carefully before starting. If you want to try other stitches not shown in this section, try holding the book upside down. Once the needle is inserted into the fabric, use the middle finger of your right hand at the fabric back to help guide the needle to the fabric front. When the needle tip appears on the fabric surface, you can easily grasp it with your left hand to continue the next stitch. If you take a class, always sit in front of the instructor to observe the stitches.

Buttonhole Stitch

Work this stitch from right to left. Come up at A and hold the thread down with your thumb. Go down at B and emerge at C. Bring the needle tip over the thread and pull into place. The bottom line formed should lie on the seam line; keep the vertical stitches straight and even.

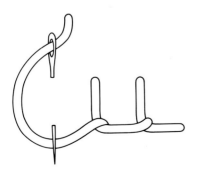
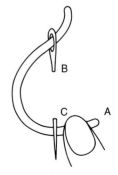

Chain Stitch

Come up at A and form a loop. Go down at B (as close to A as possible, but not into it) and emerge at C bringing the needle tip over the thread. Repeat this stitch to make a chain.

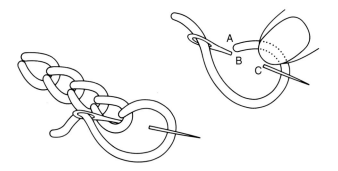

Chevron Stitch

Work the stitch from right to left along two parallel lines. Come up at A, go down at B, and emerge at C (the center of the stitch). Make a straight stitch the desired length to D, insert the needle, and emerge at E. Go down at F (equal to the length of AB) and emerge at G. Continue working, alternating from one side to the other and keeping the stitches evenly spaced.

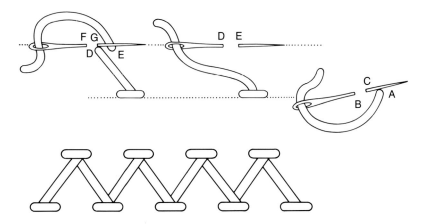

Colonial Knot

Come up at A. Work the thread to form a loop starting over the needle head and ending under the needle tip. This forms a figure "8." Hold the needle upright and pull the thread firmly around the needle. Insert the needle at B (as close to A as possible, but not into it) and hold the knot in place until the needle is worked completely through the fabric.

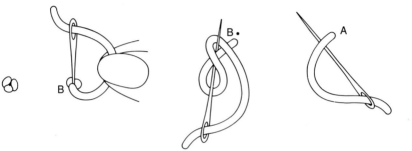

Cretan Stitch

Work this stitch, from right to left, along two parallel lines. Come up at A, go down at B, and emerge at C taking a downward vertical stitch the desired length and bringing the needle tip over the thread. Insert at D and emerge at E taking an upward vertical stitch. Be sure to keep the vertical stitches evenly spaced.

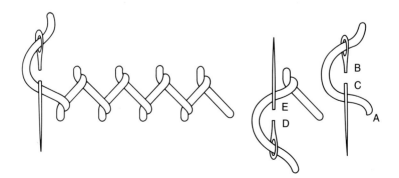

Featherstitch

Come up at A, go down at B (even with and to the right of A), and emerge at C. Alternate the stitches back and forth, working them downwards in a vertical column.

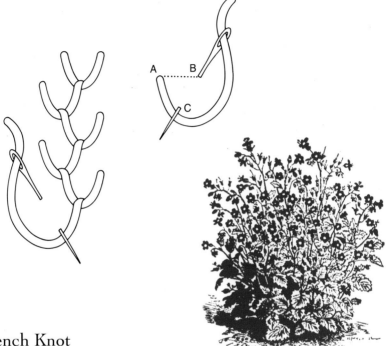

French Knot

Come up at A and wrap the thread twice around the needle. While holding the thread taut, go down at B (as close to A as possible, but not into it). Hold the knot in place until the needle is completely through the fabric.

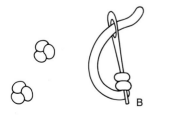
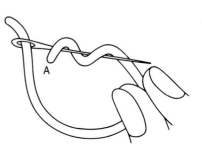

Herringbone Stitch

Work the stitch from right to left. Come up at A, go down at B, and emerge at C taking a small horizontal backstitch. Continue working, alternating from side to side.

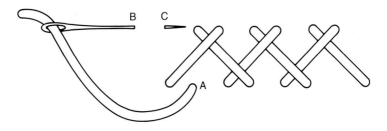

Stem Stitch

Work this stitch from right to left. Mark a line the desired length of the stem stitch. Come up at A and go down at B, making a straight stitch along the designated line; then, emerge at C (the midpoint of the previous stitch) keeping the thread below the needle.

CRAZY QUILT
COMBINATIONS

CRAZY QUILT COMBINATIONS

The beauty of a crazy quilt was always judged by the variety of stitches! It was a challenge to come up with unusual combinations and designs. The clever Victorian woman learned early on that traditional, basic embroidery stitches could be combined to produce intricate looking designs. Try using various colored threads or yarn in combination to make the stitches sparkle and look more intricate than they are.

Practice these stitches then strike out on your own. Record your combinations for later use and enjoy!

Buttonhole Stitch Variations

Pyramid
Buttonhole
+
Straight Stitch
+
French Knot

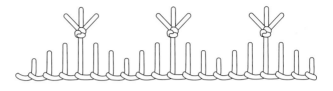

Pyramid
Buttonhole
+
French Knot
+
Lazy Daisy

Slanted
Buttonhole
+
French Knot
+
Straight Stitch

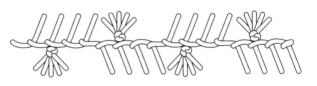

Slanted
Buttonhole
+
Lazy Daisy
+
Straight Stitch

Pyramid
Buttonhole
+
Straight Stitch
+
French Knot
+
Lazy Daisy

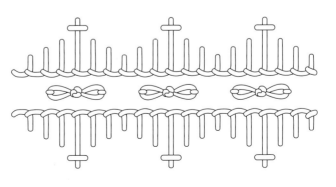

Slanted
Buttonhole
+
Straight Stitch
+
French Knot

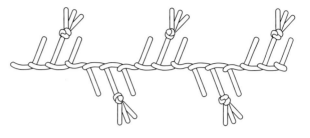

Slanted
Buttonhole
+
Straight Stitch
+
Lazy Daisy

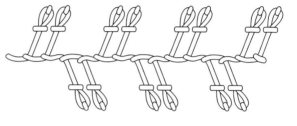

Buttonhole
+
French Knot
+
Straight Stitch
+
Lazy Daisy

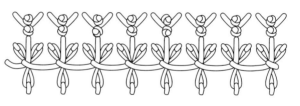

Pyramid
Buttonhole
+
Lazy Daisy
Fan

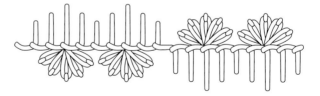

Buttonhole
+
French Knot
+
Straight Stitch

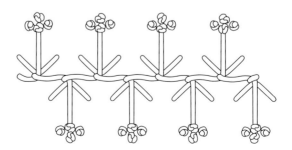

Semi-circle
Buttonhole
+
French Knot
+
Straight Stitch
Fan

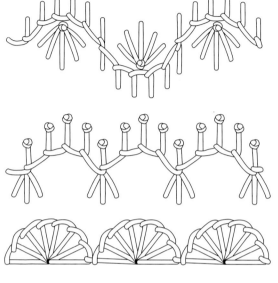

Curved
Buttonhole
+
French Knot
+
Straight Stitch
Fan

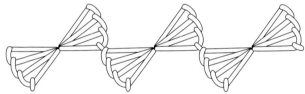

Curved
Buttonhole

Curved
Buttonhole
Bow Tie

Chain Stitch Variations

Chain Stitch
+
Straight Stitch
(Centipedes)

Chain Stitch
+
Lazy Daisy
+
Colonial Knot

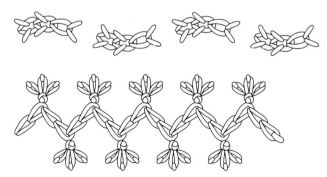

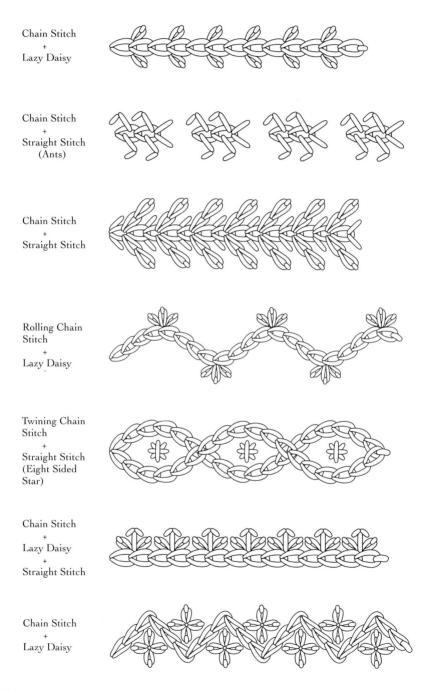

Chain Stitch
+
Lazy Daisy

Chain Stitch
+
Straight Stitch
(Ants)

Chain Stitch
+
Straight Stitch

Rolling Chain
Stitch
+
Lazy Daisy

Twining Chain
Stitch
+
Straight Stitch
(Eight Sided
Star)

Chain Stitch
+
Lazy Daisy
+
Straight Stitch

Chain Stitch
+
Lazy Daisy

Chevron Stitch Variations

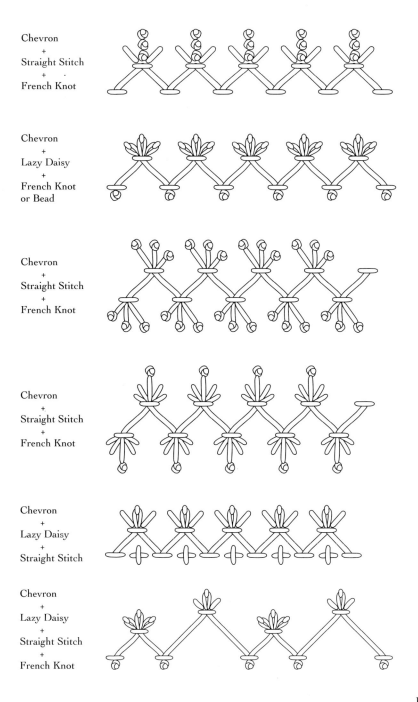

Chevron
+
Straight Stitch
+
French Knot

Chevron
+
Lazy Daisy
+
French Knot
or Bead

Chevron
+
Straight Stitch
+
French Knot

Chevron
+
Straight Stitch
+
French Knot

Chevron
+
Lazy Daisy
+
Straight Stitch

Chevron
+
Lazy Daisy
+
Straight Stitch
+
French Knot

Cretan Stitch Variations

Cretan
+
French Knot
+
Lazy Daisy

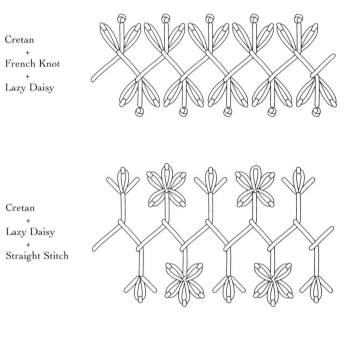

Cretan
+
Lazy Daisy
+
Straight Stitch

Overlapping
Cretan
(use two colors)

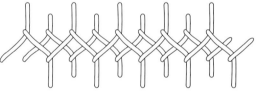

Cretan
+
French Knot
+
Straight Stitch

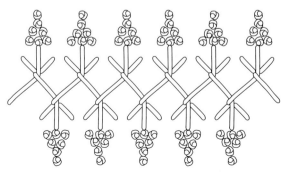

Cretan
+
Lazy Daisy
+
French Knot

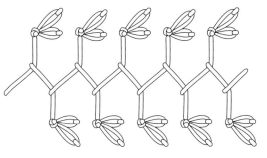

Cretan
+
Straight Stitch
+
French Knot

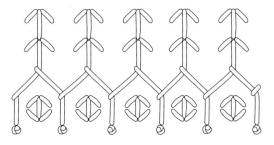

Cretan
+
Lazy Daisy
+
French Knot

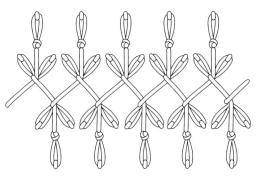

Cretan
+
Straight Stitch
+
French Knot

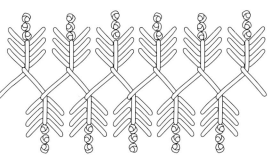

Stacked Cretan
+
Lazy Daizy
+
French Knot

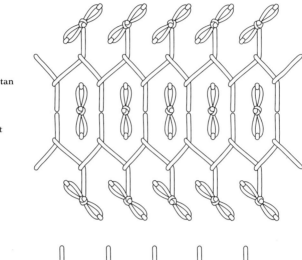

Stacked Cretan

Cretan
+
Straight Stitch
+
French Knot

Cretan
+
Straight Stitch

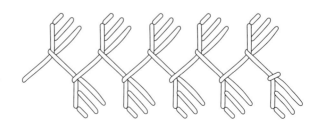

Cretan
+
Straight Stitch

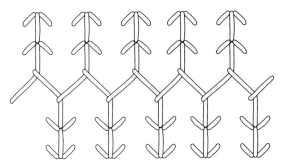

Cretan
+
Straight Stitch
+
French Knot

Cretan
+
Straight Stitch
+
Lazy Daisy

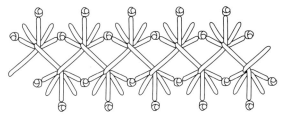

Slanted Cretan
+
Lazy Daisy
+ .
French Knot
+
Straight Stitch

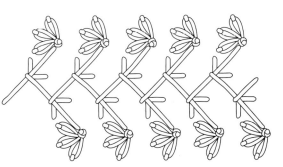

Slanted Cretan
+
Lazy Daisy
+
French Knot
+
Straight Stitch

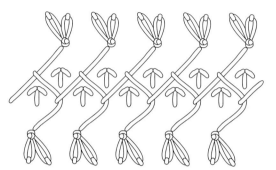

Slanted Cretan
+
Straight Stitch

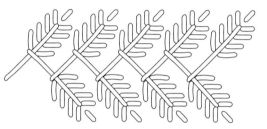

Cretan
+
Lazy Daisy
+
Straight Stitch
+
French Knot

Stacked Cretan
+
Straight Stitch
(Church Steeple)

Fan Variations

Straight Stitch
+
French Knot

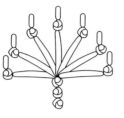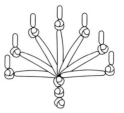

Lazy Daisy
with Long
Catch Stitch
+
Colonial Knot

Straight Stitch
+
French Knot

Straight Stitch
+
Lazy Daisy
+
French Knot

Straight Stitch
+
Lazy Daisy
+
French Knot

Featherstitch Variations

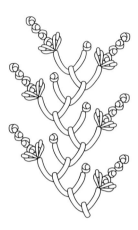

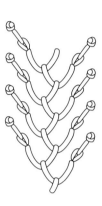

Double Featherstitch
+
French Knot
+
Lazy Daisy

Double Featherstitch
+
Lazy Daisy
+
Straight Stitch

Featherstitch
+
Lazy Daisy with
Long Catch Stitch
+
French Knot

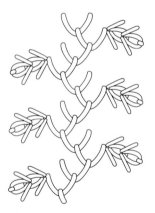

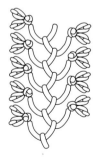

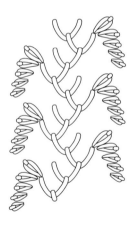

Double Featherstitch
+
Lazy Daisy
+
French Knot

Double Featherstitch
+
Lazy Daisy

Featherstitch
+
Lazy Daisy
+
French Knot

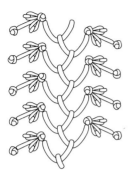

Featherstitch
+
French Knot
+
Lazy Daisy
+
Straight Stitch

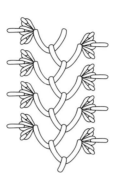

Featherstitch
+
Lazy Daisy
(Middle Lazy Daisy with
Long Catch Stitch)

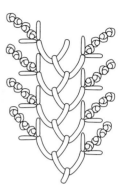

Featherstitch
+
Straight Stitch
+
French Knot

Floral Pattern Variations

Lazy Daisy
+
Colonial Knot
+
Stem Stitch

Colonial Knot
+
Lazy Daisy
+
Straight Stitch
+
French Knot
+
Stem Stitch

French Knot
+
Lazy Daisy
+
Stem Stitch

Lazy Daisy
+
Colonial Knot
+
Stem Stitch

French Knot
+
Lazy Daisy
+
Colonial Knot
+
Stem Stitch

Herringbone Stitch Variations

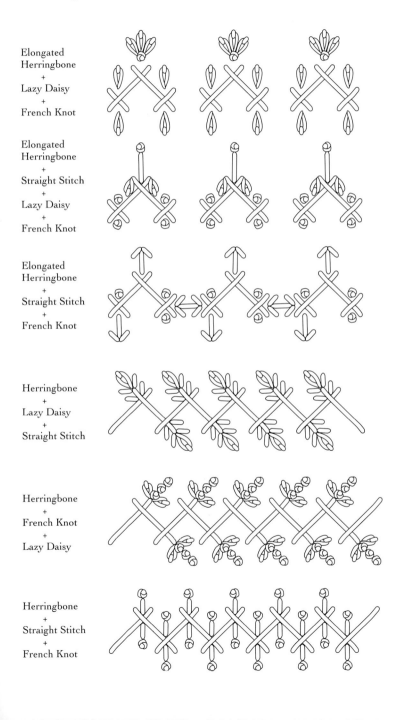

Elongated
Herringbone
+
Lazy Daisy
+
French Knot

Elongated
Herringbone
+
Straight Stitch
+
Lazy Daisy
+
French Knot

Elongated
Herringbone
+
Straight Stitch
+
French Knot

Herringbone
+
Lazy Daisy
+
Straight Stitch

Herringbone
+
French Knot
+
Lazy Daisy

Herringbone
+
Straight Stitch
+
French Knot

Elongated
Herringbone
+
Lazy Daisy
+
Straight Stitch
+
French Knot

Herringbone
+
French Knot or
Bead
+
Lazy Daizy
+
Straight Stitch

Herringbone
+
French Knot
+
Straight Stitch
Fan

Double Row
Herringbone
+
French Knot
+
Lazy Daisy
+
Straight Stitch

Double Row
Herringbone
+
Straight Stitch

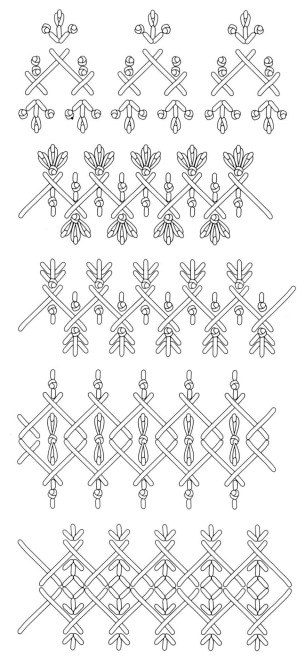

Double Row
Herringbone
+
Lazy Daisy
+
French Knot

Herringbone
+
Lazy Daisy
+
Straight Stitch
+
French Knot

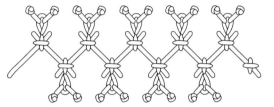

Elongated
Herringbone
+
Straight Stitch
+
French Knot
+
Lazy Daisy

Long
Herringbone
+
Straight Stitch
(Eight Sided
Star or Four
Straight Stitches
Crossed)

Long
Herringbone
+
Straight Stitch
+
French Knot

Elongated
Herringbone
+
Lazy Daisy
+
Straight Stitch
+
French Knot

Elongated
Herringbone
+
Straight Stitch
+
French Knot

Lazy Daisy Stitch Variations

Lazy Daisy
+
Colonial Knot
or Bead

Lazy Daisy
+
Straight Stitch
+
French Knot

Lazy Daisy
with Elongated
Catch Stitch
+
French Knot

Lazy Daisy
+
Colonial Knot
or Bead

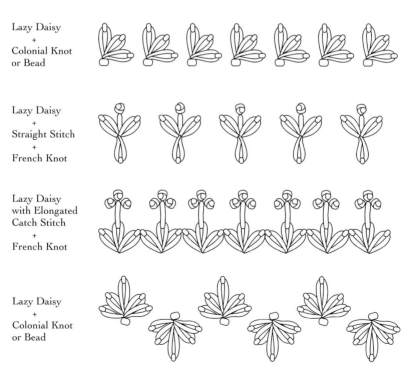

Lazy Daisy

Lazy Daisy
+
Straight Stitch
+
French Knot

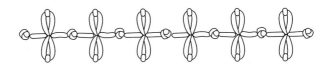

Lazy Daisy
+
Colonial Knot
+
Straight Stitch

Lazy Daisy
+
Straight Stitch
+
French Knot

Lazy Daisy
with Double
Catch Stitch
+
Straight Stitch

Lazy Daisy
+
Straight Stitch
+
French Knot

Lazy Daisy
+
Straight Stitch

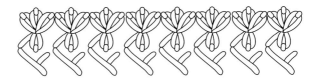

Lazy Daisy
+
Straight Stitch

Lazy Daisy
+
Straight Stitch
+
French Knot or
Bead

Lazy Daisy
+
Straight Stitch
+
French Knot

Lazy Daisy
+
Straight Stitch
+
French Knot
+
Bead

Lazy Daisy
+
Straight Stitch

Lazy Daisy
+
Straight Stitch

Lazy Daisy
+
Straight Stitch
+
French Knot

Lazy Daisy
+
Colonial Knot

Lazy Daisy
+
Straight Stitch

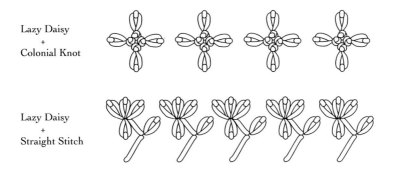

Special Combination Variations

Herringbone
+
Straight Stitch
(on top)
+
Cretan
(on the bottom)

Chevron
+
Cretan

Chevron
(on top)
+
Herringbone
+
Straight Stitch
(on the bottom)

Straight Stitch
+
Lazy Daisy

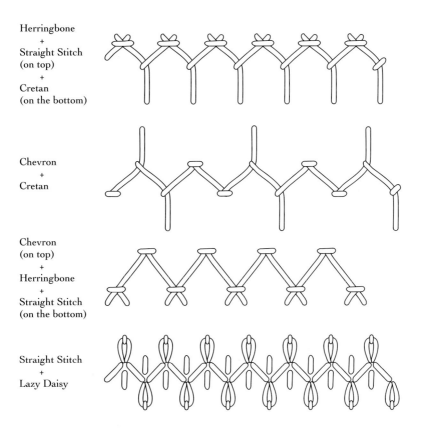

Chevron
+
Cretan
+
Straight Stitch
+
French Knot
+
Lazy Daisy

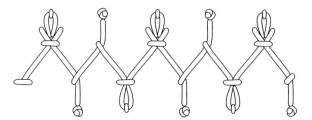

Buttonhole
+
Herringbone
+
French Knot
+
Straight Stitch
+
Lazy Daisy

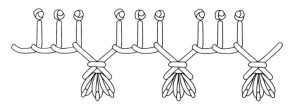

Herringbone
+
Cretan
+
Straight Stitch
+
French Knot
+
Lazy Daisy

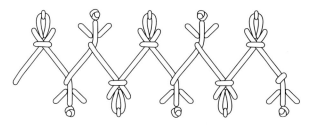

Herringbone
+
Straight Stitch
+
Lazy Daisy
(on top)
+
Chevron
(on the bottom)

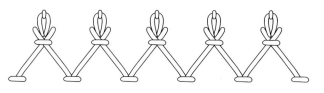

Cretan
+
Buttonhole
+
Straight Stitch
+
French Knot

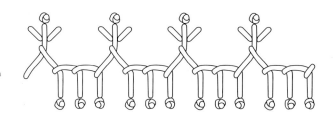

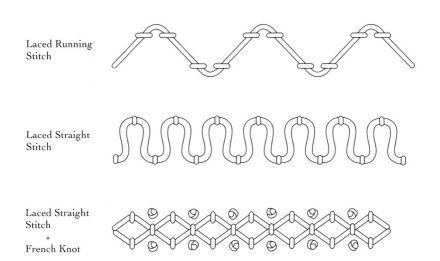

Laced Running
Stitch

Laced Straight
Stitch

Laced Straight
Stitch
+
French Knot

Web Variations

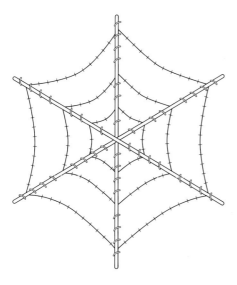

Six Intersecting Spokes
with Couched Thread

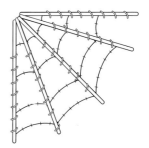

Corner Web with
Couched Thread

Spider
Chain Stitch
+
Two Beads

Six Spoked Web
with Continuous and
Couched Threads

Zigzag Pattern Variations

Zigzag Chain
Stitch

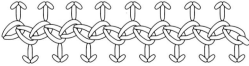

Zigzag Chain
Stitch
+
Straight Stitch
+
French Knot

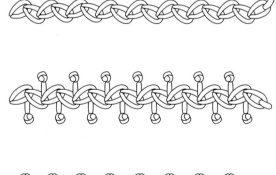

Zigzag Chain
Stitch
+
Straight Stitch

Zigzag
+
French Knot

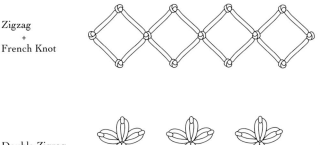

Double Zigzag
+
French Knot
+
Lazy Daisy

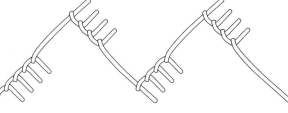

Zigzag
+
Lazy Daisy
+
Colonial Knot

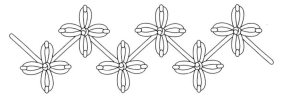

Zigzag
Buttonhole

Zigzag
Buttonhole
+
Lazy Daisy
+
French Knot

Zigzag
Buttonhole
+
Straight Stitch
Fan
+
French Knot

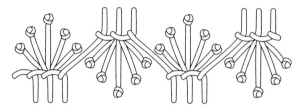

Zigzag
Buttonhole
+
French Knot
+
Lazy Daisy

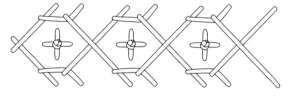

Zigzag
Buttonhole
+
Lazy Daisy
+
Cross Stitch

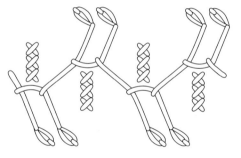

Zigzag
Buttonhole
+
Straight Stitch
+
French Knot

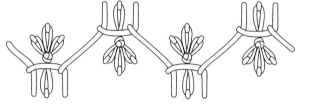

Zigzag
Buttonhole
+
French Knot
+
Lazy Daisy

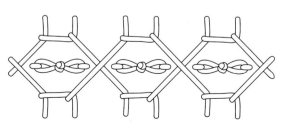

Zigzag
+
Lazy Daisy
+
Straight Stitch

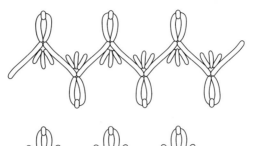

Zigzag
+
Straight Stitch
+
Lazy Daisy

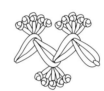

Zigzag Chain
Stitch
+
Straight Stitch
+
French Knot

Zigzag Chain
Stitch
+
Straight Stitch
+
French Knot

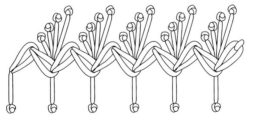

FREE-FORM STITCHERY

ere are a few free-form pieces I've done over the last two years. I thought you would enjoy seeing the process I use to get to the finished product. I keep a sketchbook of ideas, some may never be used or perhaps will be incorporated into a collage piece. My sketchbook is full of notes and addresses of people I've met along the way. Get in the habit of carrying a sketchbook with you and you'll never regret it…mine becomes a visual diary for each passing year. A tiny watercolor set provides all the color I need to jog my memory. A beat-up old camera is my constant companion and I'm always looking for that perfect photograph (so far it has eluded me, but half the joy in photography is the search for that special photograph).

Pictures in magazines, poetry, and short stories may become the seed that flourishes into a finished landscape. I cut these out and keep them in file folders according to subject. Music is another great source of inspiration for me. A cowboy ballad by Ian Tyson always brings pictures of my Alberta home flooding back to me. A song by Roger Whitaker has me perched on a rocky ledge overlooking the Blue Mountains of Australia, the sound track of "The Little Mermaid" has me 50 feet under the sea, a Dolly Parton song about Tennessee brings memories of those special friends in the Smoky Mountains, and the song "Shine on Harvest Moon"…well that's another story!

Just realize that inspiration is everywhere and keep a record of it all.

FREE FORM
STITCHERY

GARDEN MEMORIES

9" x 14"; private collection

My goal is to introduce the quilting world and needlework industry to each other and to show my students how to collage various techniques into needle art and one-of-a-kind artwork.

This small cottage scene uses crazy quilting, Victorian stitches, painting on cross-stitch cloth, silk ribbon embroidery, lace collage, wool embroidery, beading, ruched ribbons, pen and ink sketching, crewel embroidery, folded ribbon, the addition of buttons and charms, and burning techniques. Whew! Quite a list, but when you think of all the needleart techniques you've learned over the years, you probably know how to do a lot of them. Why not combine them for extra visual and textural interest? Free yourself of all those "learned" rules and join in the adventure of free-form embroidery.

I chose the fabrics for my free-form embroidery from liberty prints and a variety of sky blue fabrics. I used the busy floral prints for the garden area and the solids for the sky.

While making a template from milky template plastic, I decided on a vertical shape, then cut this shape from the plastic. This allowed me to draw the "window" around my piece, then burn down to the drawn line.

I transferred this line to the Hardanger cross-stitch cloth, then drew my cottage scene within the lines.

Using colored permanent marker, I outlined the cottage, path, and brick wall. I painted the sky and trees using watercolor paints.

Once the fabric dried, I painted in the cottage path and walk. Cross hatching and more detail were added (after drying again) with permanent pens. The painted piece was then basted into the window opening.

I decided earlier to have the light coming from right to left. The path spills out into the crazy quilt area, creating depth through color and texture.

Next came the Victorian stitches. Using similar colors and fine silk threads, I used single and double featherstitches in the sky (see detail below) to create a sense of movement and form a background for the busier garden area. I let the watercolor paints blend out onto the crazy quilt sky for a better visual effect.

Every seam line in the crazy quilted garden area was covered with a variety of crazy quilt stitches worked with a selection of mohair, wool, and silk yarns. The next step was to lay down ribbons, lace, and braided trims. More embroidery was added to hold these pieces in place and to create more depth.

In order to create a sense of distance, I purposely kept the embroidery in the cottage area small and delicate, making a conscious effort to enlarge the stitches and to use heavier material in the foreground, so the viewer has a sense of traveling down the garden path. Found items, such as ombre ribbon, antique flower buttons, pearls, glass, and metal butterflies, add more detail to the foreground.

If you lay down lace leaf shapes, leave the edges loose. The lace wall extends from the brick wall in the painted area since the lace edges are folded and left loose at the top.

Straight stitches create a good pathway. Make long and short straight stitches using variegated yarn for extra interest. Lay down ombre ribbon in a jumble to create a garden effect as in the right, lower corner of garden (see detail above).

For the cottage wall with climbing roses use a single strand of floss for the double and triple feather-stitches. The roses are single-stranded French knots. To get more depth, use heavier yarn and colonial knots for the climbing roses on the front of the cottage. Also, twisted, variegated wire ribbon makes a wonderful textural background for beading, doo-dads, and folded flowers. Don't be afraid to mix materials such as yarn and silk ribbon.

COTTAGE GARDENS

How I Love Them!

CLIMBing ROSES
FEATHER STITCH & FRENch K.NOTs

BRIAR ROSE

— STRAIGHT STITCHES

"I say, Can you tell me what Kind of plant That is?" "CAN'T say That I can GUY!"

CRAZY QUILTING pale blue SKY

LACE?

PAINT A picture ONTO CROSS-STITCH CLOTH . . . . . CUT a hole OUT OF a square of crazy quilting
Burn The edges
This becomes a picture with in a picture. . . .
The Path Travels From The House out of The opening and INTO The Foreground

Burned edge

Light comes From Th

STRAIGHT STITCHES FOR PATH

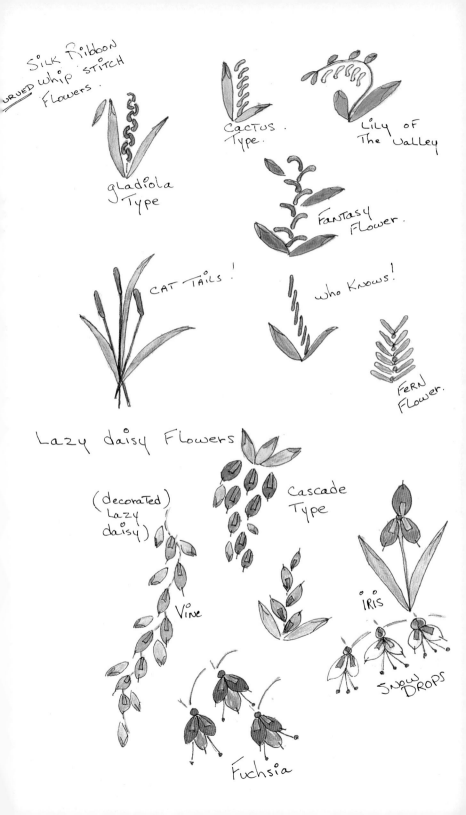

Silk Ribbon
CURVED WHIP STITCH
Flowers.

Cactus.
Type.

Lily of
The Valley

gladiola
Type

Fantasy
Flower.

CAT TAILS!

who Knows!

Fern.
Flower.

Lazy daisy Flowers

(decorated)
Lazy
daisy)

Cascade
Type

Vine

Iris

Snow
DROPS

Fuchsia

GUARDIANS OF THE MERMAID GARDEN

6" x 14"; courtesy: Madeleine J. Montaño

I learned to snorkel and scuba dive a few years ago, and I haven't been the same since! I am thoroughly convinced the gods have reserved the ocean and seabeds for their own private gardens and pleasure!

My favorite fish are the tiny tropicals that live among the coral branches. These colorful, fanciful warriors guard their territory with such ferocity that something the size of a diver can't scare them off! (I admire their courage even more than their brilliant mantles of color.)

A piece of dyed cotton by Mickey Lawler of Sky Dye Fabrics was the inspiration for this piece. I laid in three quilting lines with metallic thread to indicate depth and sea bubbles. Next, I applied spark organdy and silk ribbon: first twisted, then held down with beads (to represent seaweed). To create twisted ribbon, anchor the raw edge of the ribbon to the fabric. At equal intervals, twist the ribbon to form an angle. Come up with the needle from underneath the fabric and tack this ribbon angle down with a bead or French knot. Be sure to anchor the stitches securely to the back of your work. By twisting silk knitting yarn with pearl cotton, then couching it down with metallic thread, I was able to come up with great sea grass. Two colors of variegated 1/4" (4 mm) silk ribbon were runched on a metallic thread for another type of seaweed.

Using a free-form featherstitch, seaweed forms were laid in with variegated silk ribbon and yarns. I used variegated ribbons, made by Kathy Sorrensen of Island Fibers, exclusively throughout this piece. (Which brings up a point — know your limitations! I do not enjoy dyeing fabrics and ribbon, so I barter or buy from artists who do it well. I'm also very careful to acknowledge their products in my work!)

Next, 2" of organza ribbon was tacked loosely in place along the foreground. Textural shapes were then embroidered in place using silk ribbon for the Montano knots, whip stitches, and colonial knots. Freshwater pearls, sea coral, and turquoise were sewn along the knots for added interest.

And last, but not least, are the fish. I purchased these carved turquoise and oyster shell fetishes from an Indian friend in New Mexico. A fetish holds the spirit of the bird, fish, or animal who has given up its life to become food for the hunter. Rather appropriate for this piece, I thought.

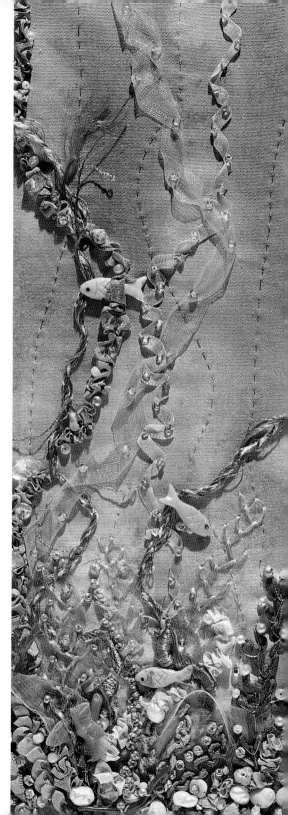

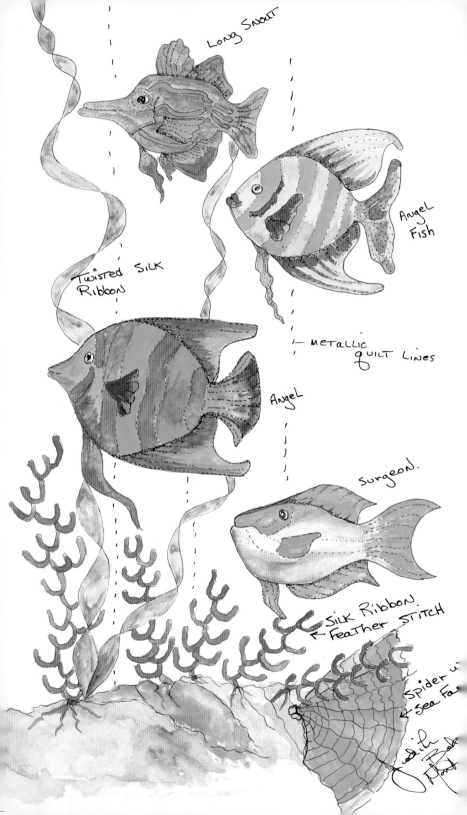

Long Snout

Angel Fish

Twisted Silk Ribbon

metallic quilt lines

Angel

Surgeon.

Silk Ribbon. Feather Stitch

Spider w. Sea Fa

Judith Baker Montano

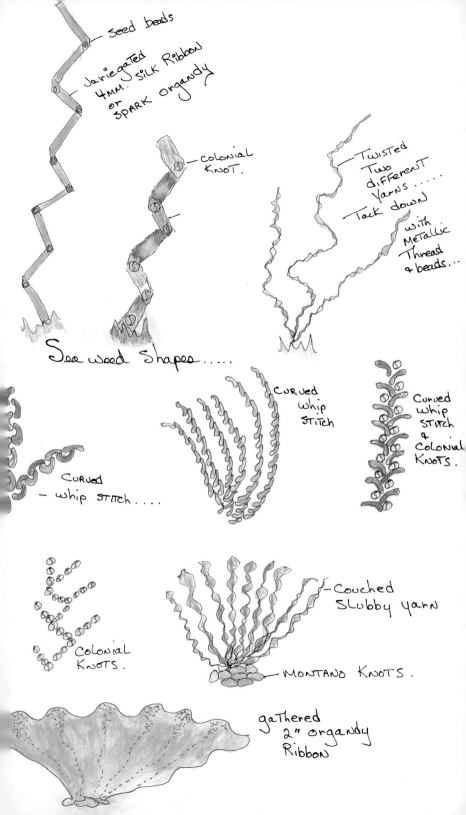

Seed beads

Variegated 4mm. silk Ribbon or SPARK organdy

Colonial Knot.

Twisted Two different Yarns ..... Tack down

with Metallic Thread & beads...

Sea weed Shapes.....

Curved whip Stitch

Curved whip Stitch & Colonial Knots.

Curved - whip stitch....

Colonial Knots.

Couched Slubby yarn

MONTANO KNOTS.

gathered 2" organdy Ribbon

STORM AT NORAH HEAD BEACH

8 ¹/₂" x 7 ¹/₂"; courtesy: J. Montano

One of my favorite hobbies is photography and once in awhile I come up with a great photo. While in New South Wales, Australia, I was driving along the coastline and a terrible storm was rolling in. The cloud formation and late afternoon sun created unbelievable colors in the sky— the shading varied from mauve to peach to blue gray. I stopped the car and raced down to the beach, shooting pictures as I ran. Thirty-six shots later I only had one good picture, but it was well worth the effort. I wanted to commemorate this scene in fabric, so I made this small porthole picture for myself. It hangs in the hallway of my home.

There are only four main pieces in this small picture: the sky, the ocean, the foreground, and the pathway. These are all silk fabrics that have been painted over with watercolor paints. The fence posts and white waves were made by burning the edges with a candle flame. Silk gets a lovely brown edge, almost like a drawn edge when burnt. Yvonne Porcella taught me this method and it opened a door for a whole new avenue of expression.

Note: All fabrics will burn! Polyesters get a crisp, hard edge; cottons smolder and have a brown edge; and Ultrasuede® gets a black, melted edge. Be sure to work safely. For extra protection, keep the candle in a holder and keep both in a pan of water.

The grass was laid in with straight stitches — piled one on top of the other — using silk and wool variegated yarns. The darker shades form the background, with lighter and finer threads coming to the foreground. Chain stitches were used in the foreground along with French and Montano knots. The wood posts and gray silk fabrics were cut and burned, then held down with straight and chain stitches. I worked hard to blend the threads into the gray shades. The metal rod posts are long straight stitches of silk, wrapped with white yarn. The barbed wire is a single strand of floss couched down with the same thread.

I indicated the pathway with a featherstitch of various threads; the darker shades of stitches create shadow along the edge of the path. Notice that the metallic copper threads add a glint of sunlight on the path and vegetation.

This little piece brings me a lot of joy. Not only did I enjoy creating it, but I never walk down the hall without pausing to look at it. I find myself back at Norah Head Beach, running along the path with the sand dragging at my feet, the sea air smelling salty and damp, and the wind whistling in accompaniment to the pounding surf while the sun dances and weaves among the storm clouds…aah, memories are made of this!

The horizon line of water — (Lakes, ocean, inlets, mud puddles, sea, ponds) always lies in a straight line! (horizontal that is!)

grass shapes

← CURVED OUTLINE STITCHES.

STRAIGHT STITCH

Chain stitch

← FLY STITCH

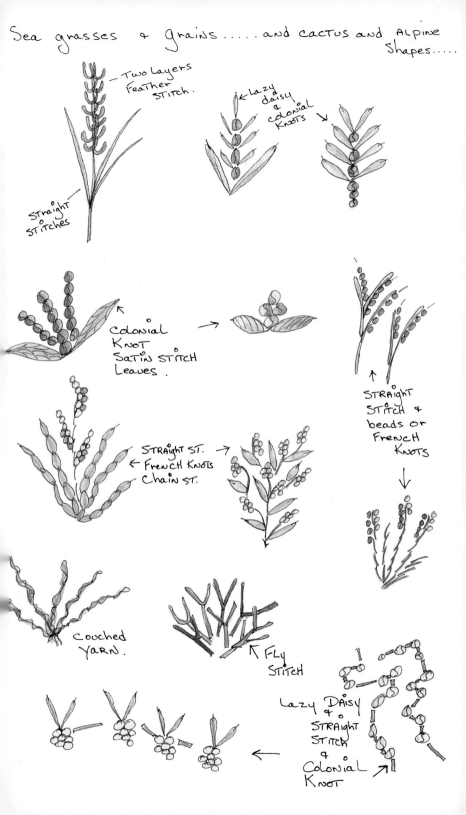

Sea grasses & grains..... and cactus and Alpine Shapes.....

Two Layers Feather Stitch.

Straight Stitches

Lazy Daisy & colonial Knots

Colonial Knot Satin Stitch Leaves.

Straight Stitch & beads or French Knots

Straight St. French Knots Chain St.

Couched Yarn.

Fly Stitch

Lazy Daisy & Straight Stitch & Colonial Knot

GRANDPA WAS A BIG, BIG MAN

9" x 12"; private collection

When my mother was fourteen and my uncle was a little boy, they lost their father: my dear Grandpa. This photo of my uncle leaning back against Grandpa's legs, as though Grandpa was a big sturdy tree, always brings certain memories to me. Remember when we were all little and the grownups looked so big to us, almost like giants? Now I'm a grownup, but I don't feel very "big"!

Using the Australian photo transfer method, I transferred my photos to parachute silk and then aged them in coffee. I chose to work in dusty tones to evoke a feeling of age, of time passing.

The Victorian photograph was cut at angles into five sections. It is the "centerpiece" for centerpiece crazy quilt methods (refer to either *Crazy Quilt Handbook* or *Crazy Quilt Odyssey*). I wanted a variety of shapes and sizes in order to heavily collage various needlework techniques over it. I like to work in the crazy quilt method, as it is the most "painterly" of all the quilting methods. You must think as an artist while working in this technique.

The muslin base becomes your canvas. The chosen fabrics are the paints and there is no pattern—only your imagination is your guide. As there is no set pattern for crazy quilting, the outer perimeter of the muslin becomes a guideline, then the fabrics are laid down (right sides together, folded over, then pressed) in a pleasing design. Remember, this layer of fabrics is only the first layer of color. Various needlework techniques will be laid over the layers to create visual interest.

When I started this piece, I wanted to create a sense of time, of bygone days. The Victorian picture of the little boy (see detail at left) with the bow and arrow is from Australia; it has such a nostalgic feel to it. Various types of lace were "antiqued" (page 162) with coffee or tea, before they were added to the fabric. All the seams were decorated with Victorian stitches, using a variety of threads and ribbons.

A large spray of silk ribbon embroidery acts as the focal point for the picture. Several satin concertina roses were sewn in place, then surrounded with a variety of 4mm silk flowers. (Every variety of flower has a different colored green leaf in this project, so have a good supply of greens in your collection before you start stitching!)

Ruched or twisted silk ribbon adds interest and a soft texture to this piece. The free-form featherstitches become shrubbery to highlight the picture of father and son. By working the stitches into the photograph, it helps to blend all the units.

Note: When using buttons and charms, try working them into clusters for more interest, instead of using them randomly throughout your piece.

"When gazing into the eyes of a lover..... It is best to see the eyes of a friend!"
JUDITH

MUM

DAD

grandad VAN WINKLE

UNCLE DONNY.

grandpa & grandma Baker

Shantzie (granma)

My grandpa was a farmer and he said "Fly, stretch your wings, expand your mind.... but never forget your roots....cherish your roots." JAMES ALLEN BAKER.

"SWEET MEMORIES" OR
"FAILED FEATHERS…"

9" x 12"; private collection

I made this collage as a companion piece to "Grandpa was a Big, Big Man." It was a challenge to create a nostalgic piece using the same methods as "Grandpa," but with contemporary pictures.

I had a lovely cat named Lofty, for the simple reason that he lived in the loft of the barn and preferred this to our house. He was a gentleman in every sense of the word, except for one unforgivable habit: he would catch birds of all types then bring them to me, much like an offering to the "Lady of the Manor." Upon being laid at my feet, the bird—unharmed, but rigid with fear—would revive suddenly and fly off into my house! The whole family would then get into the act of "rescuing the victim"—putting the poor bird into a further state of shock. Happily, all the birds survived and Lofty lived to be an old gentleman cat.

The centerpiece photo is of my children, Madeleine and Jason Montaño, at the ages of two and five. The challenge was to use the same materials and wire ribbon, or the same amount of lace and findings. Lofty is framed with featherstitched shrubbery and bird fetishes. Antique mother-of-pearl buttons peek out of the twisted wire ribbon. Ruched silk ribbon and a spray of satin and silk ribbon flowers meander along the centerpiece photograph to give depth and texture to the piece.

This piece is worked in light dusty shades…watercolor paint was added to the silk photographs to further blend into the collage.

Muriel and Harry Hays
were my Grandparents
"and They were good to me"
Judith
1993

Muriel

RECOLLECTIONS OF LOVE

28" x 34"; courtesy: Senator Daniel P. Hays
photo courtesy of D.M., Trails End

At some point in our lives we are confronted with the loss of a loved one. While following the prescribed grief process, we all handle our sadness in different ways.

Out of pain and grief comes creativity and healing, and that is why some artists create their greatest works with a broken heart...such is "Recollections of Love" for me. I was raised from the age of fourteen by my godparents. They adored me and the love was returned to them tenfold. My godfather died thirteen years ago and my reaction to that great void was to create a pictorial quilt in his memory. When my god-mother died in the fall of 1992, I was shocked at the overwhelming grief. For solace I turned to my needlework and created "Recollections of Love" from a collection of their personal belongings: ties, buttons, hankies, scarves, clothing, and jewelry.

My goal was to create a "Chinook" effect across the Alberta foothills scene. A Chinook is a warm, westerly wind created by the ocean currents around Japan. It blows over the Rocky Mountains, transform-ing a cold, blustery snow-packed Alberta day into a day filled with rivulets of running water, warm, soft breezes, and mud—lots of it! I wanted to create the view as seen from their ranch house, with the Chinook of memories blowing across the sky in a crazy quilt collage.

Using the Australian photo method, I started with several senti-mental photographs transferred to parachute silk. These photo memo-ries cover a span of fifty years.

Australian Photo Method

Materials

- ♦ a photocopy of a photo or picture (it must be a photocopy made with dry toner, not a laser or color copy print)
- ♦ pure gum turpentine
- ♦ blotting paper
- ♦ large metal spoon
- ♦ cotton balls
- ♦ natural fabric such as cotton batiste or silk (no polyester)

Process

1. Place the blotting paper on a table. Lay the silk (after it has been well pressed and is wrinkle free) down on the blotting paper. Lay the photocopy face down on the silk.

2. Dip the cotton ball in the turpentine (don't get it soppy wet) and rub the back of the photocopy until it becomes opaque.

3. Take the spoon in one hand and hold the photocopy firmly in place with the other hand. Rub the back of the photocopy very hard with the spoon.

4. Carefully lift up a corner of the paper to check the image. If the image is faint, rub on a bit more turpentine and burnish with the spoon again.

5. Remove the photocopy. Iron the image into the silk. You may color the image with watercolors or acrylic paints.

I had to decide on the tone or shading of colors to use. Since my mementos acted as the paints in my palette, I laid them out then decided to use a light, dusty rose and teal as the two main colors.

The white laces and hankies were toned down with either coffee or tea (coffee gives a soft tan or brownish shade; tea gives a pink shade). After sewing the pieces, I noticed there were some light areas that seemed as if they jumped forward (remember, lights come forward and darks recede). My original plan was to move from top to bottom, shading light to dark, so I painted the offending areas with acrylic paints.

Antiquing method (using coffee or tea) — make a strong solution of coffee or tea and dip the fabric you want "aged" into it. Leave for at least ten minutes. Rinse the fabric in cold water, then finish rinsing in a solution of $1/3$ part vinegar to $2/3$ parts water. Air dry the fabric then iron to set the color.

Adding punch needle embroidery—in the far left corner I needle-punched the design for texture and to indicate a tree line.

Stitching fir trees—use three shades of green. Start with the darkest shade and make large free-form featherstitches (see sketch on page 166). Lay the second shade of green over the previous stitches, working these stitches a bit smaller. Finish by using the lightest green on top, creating even smaller, more detailed stitches.

Enhancing landscapes — crazy quilt landscapes can be enhanced with trees, shrubs, and ground cover that are embroidered with a combination of stitches. Each country has trees that are unique and typical to its region. Australia has the beautiful gum tree. Canada has the maple tree. Japan is home of the bonsai and cherry tree. The United States hosts the evergreen and the mighty oak.

Trunks of trees can be made with a satin stitch or a combination of outline stitches and chain stitches. Lay the chain stitches down side by side. Shade the trunk with a variety of colors (lights come forward, darks recede). Leaves and small branches can be made with free-form featherstitching, a maidenhair stitch, fly stitch, or cretan stitch. Punch needle embroidery with both thread and ribbon gives an excellent foliage effect. Work all other embroidery first to hold the layers together, then punch in the leaves or shrubbery.

Here are some stitching ideas for specific trees and plants:

Bonsai Evergreen — the rugged, twisted trunk is made of chain stitches laid side by side. The branches are free-form featherstitches. The needles are embroidered with medium-looped punch needle.

Canadian Maple — the maple trunk is embroidered with outline stitches. The branches are free-form featherstitches. Leaves can be worked in smaller free-form featherstitches or medium-looped punch needle.

Cherry Tree — the cherry tree, like many flowering trees (crabapple, apple, peach, crepe myrtle) is full and round. The trunk can be outlined with a stem stitch and filled in with chain stitches. Leaves can be free-form featherstitches or punch needle. Add the flowers in the form of beads or ribbon punch needle.

Evergreen — rugged trunks are made with chain stitches and outline stitches laid side by side. The branches slope downward. The pine needles are embroidered with long-looped punch needle.

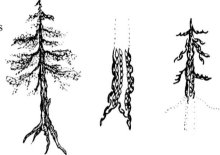

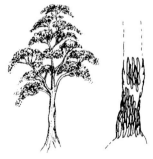

Gum Tree — one characteristic in common of the many gum tree varieties is that the leaves cluster up high at the end of long branches. Many types have unusual peeling trunks. The trunks can be embroidered with satin stitch; the leaves with punch needle.

Weeping Willow — the graceful weeping willow is worked with long and short satin stitches for the trunk and outline stitches for the long branches. The leaves are upside-down featherstitches.

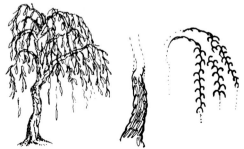

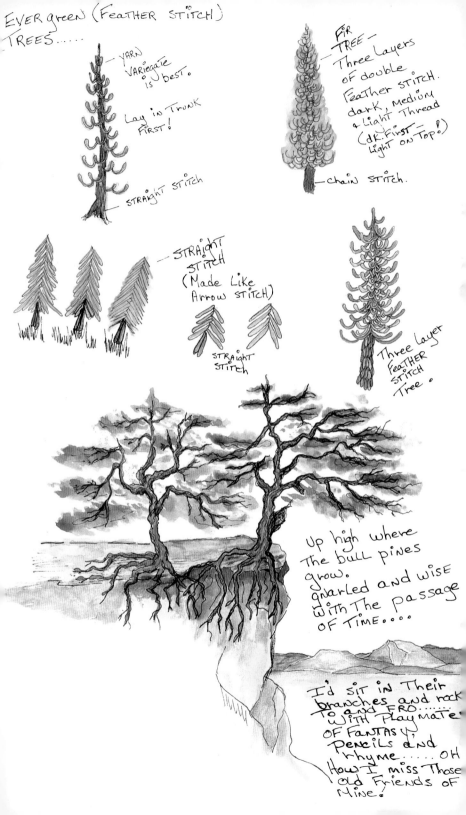

EVERGREEN (FEATHER STITCH)
TREES......

— YARN
VARIEGATE
IS best.

Lay in TRUNK
FIRST!

STRAIGHT STITCH

FIR
TREE —
Three Layers
OF double
FEATHER STITCH.
dark, MEDIUM
& Light Thread
(dk. FIRST —
Light ON TOP!)

— chain STITCH.

— STRAIGHT
STITCH
(Made Like
Arrow STITCH)

STRAIGHT
STITCH

Three Layer
FEATHER
STITCH
Tree.

Up high where
The bull pines
grow.
gnarled and wise
with The passage
OF TIME....

I'd sit in Their
branches and rock
To and FRO.....
with Playmate
OF FANTASY
PENCILS and
rhyme......OH
How I miss Those
Old Friends of
MINE!

Silk Ribbon
Collages
For
Recollections
of Love:

To be used
with Fabric
Photos ....

"good Night,
My Love:
The Shadows
gently Fall;
The Stars Above
Are watching
over all"....
(ah The old
songs said it
best).....or
is it That I'm
older now and
I appreciate
The past?.

Jolly Joker Pansy

Pansies Always
Appear pleased
To see you!!

(Use The Chinook winds
To create a cloud of
Memories).....
"And a chinook would
blow in.....like a
Savior and just blow
away all the grim
Memories of winter"
rancher near
Bragg Creek.

"Be yourself
is About
The worst
Advise you
Can give To
Some people"
Mark
Twain....
(Ahmen
To
That)!

And I Looked up To
See The Canadian Flag
at half Mast .....(above
Those beloved evergreen
Trees).... and I Knew
They were Forever gone........

Keith
93

JUST OVER THAT HILL
IS MY HOME

26" x 32"; private collection

Indian summer in Alberta, Canada is a special time. My beloved ranching foothills are alive with fall colors...one last display before the first snow fall puts it all to rest.

Because I want the viewer to recognize this particular area, I worked from a photograph taken in late afternoon light (when the colors are warm and the shadows are long). Using a grid system, I enlarged the mountains and foothills to the desired size then traced them onto paper. I made pattern shapes from the paper, adding an ⅛" seam line. This allowed me an extra ⅛" to burn around the edges. If I held the fabric to a candle flame, I was able to create a more realistic mountain and hill edge on the fabric—and a recognizable scene.

All the fabrics in this piece are silk and silk blends. The findings are western in theme, such as fetishes, bear claw, and natural stone. The sky fabric is a purchased piece, enhanced with watercolor paint.

The crazy quilt area in the lower right-hand corner was a real challenge because it represents a field of ripe grain. The lines had to run horizontally, yet that was an impossibility, so I had to achieve the effect with texture and embroidery lines.

The double and triple featherstitches in the seam lines help to create texture. The plant formations are stitched with a variety of variegated yarns, such as wool, mohair, and silk.

Stitching tree roots—many times I've stood in front of a cut bank, and am amazed at the design created by shrub and tree roots. I was able to re-create this effect by unraveling eight-stranded variegated silk threads. The variegations create a good shadow effect. Feathers from an old Victorian hat decoration helped create a root texture, as well as silk ribbon Montano knots.

Using wire ribbon —this versatile variegated ribbon comes in several widths and color variations. It can be twisted or pushed into a mass of folds and texture. I often use it in the foreground to create a deeper sense of distance.

Creating wrinkled fabrics — I wanted to create lots of texture in the crazy quilted area. I did this by sewing a much larger piece of fabric into a smaller area by wetting the fabric and pressing the wrinkles with a steam iron. I left the wrinkles loose up until the embroidery section, then re-worked the area with "catch" stitches such as the fly stitch, straight stitch, Montano knot, and French knot.

Creating pleated fabric — I placed a piece of fabric on the muslin, pleated it, and tacked the pleats in place with running stitches (see detail above). The other crazy quilt fabrics, when sewn down, also hold the pleats in place.

Using paint — once everything was sewn in place, I realized some of the hills were too light. With watercolor paints, I "grayed" the fabrics down and added shadows to the largest hill.

Tree Roots
Unravel 8 or
12 STRANDED SILK
Floss ..... couch the
single strands
Matching Thread.
(VariGates work well)

pleated Area

Deep wrinkles

CRAZY QUILT SECTION
USE Mohair yarn and wool
For Feather stitch
grass and shrubs.

YARN
Shrubs.

SILK RIBBON
Japanese Ribbo
STITCH.

CROWS ARE
The Messengers.

FLY STITCH
For TEXTURE

Feather
STITCH grass

C.G. AREA
gold, green
orange
rust.

YARN
FANTASY
Flowers.

tucked Ribbon
in pleated silk
To form rockery
and grain shape

Seam LiNE

ALBERTA'S OWN

Feather stitch Bushes.

NOVEMBER 28-94   7:34 A.M

Today I lost my beloved
horse LEO T-BAR TWIST.
(He was a PRINCE among.
horses and my friend.

LACE Doilies
ADD Texture
To crazy quilting
collages

BUTTONS.......

BUTTONS
Beads
and charms are
best when added
in clusters......

BUTTON
FLOWER

BEADS

LIFE IS LIKE AN ONION
You Peel off
one layer at a time.....
and sometimes you weep!"   Beads.
CARL Sandburg

Think of me…
> When dark clouds hang in curtains of design
>> along the far horizon
> When dove gray shadows dance and weave
>> in harmony with a shy and fleeting sun

Think of me
> When crimson red to purple hues of dawn
>> caress the mountain pines
> When soothing light adds shadow
>> deep along the valleys, the hills, and timber line

Think of me
> When wispy ribbon streaks of white
>> hang in azure noon time skies
> To create a magic springboard for the diving, gliding hawk
>> up high beyond the rise

Think of me
> When distant rolling hills of home
>> call the sun god back to rest
> When the soaring peaks beyond wear crystal shafts of light
>> upon their rugged breast

Think of me
> When viewing God's canvas of the night.
> Feel the soft, caressing breeze
>> upon your cheek
> And smile, when you hear the calling of the crow.
>> "Please think of me,
>>> think of me,
>>>> of me,
>>>>> …me."
>>>>> *—Judith*

BIBLIOGRAPHY

Coats & Clark. *100 Embroidery Stitches*. New York, N. Y.: Ballantine Books, 1981

Montano, Judith Baker. *The Art of Silk Ribbon Embroidery*, Lafayette, CA: C&T Publishing, 1993.

_____. *Crazy Quilt Odyssey, Adventures in Victorian Needlework*. Lafayette, CA: C&T Publishing, 1991

_____. *The Crazy Quilt Handbook*. Lafayette, CA: C&T Publishing, 1988

Nichols, Marion. *Encyclopedia of Embroidery Stitches, Including Crewel*. New York, NY: Dover Publications, 1974.